Show me

CW00538874

WordPerfect 6
A Visual Guide to the Basics
Jennifer Flynn

File Edit View Layout Tools

1   2   3   4   5   6

New
Open
Retrieve...
Close
Save
Save As...

File Manager...
Master Document
Compare Documents

re-of-the-a
h can do
rfec
g p
y be
may
yout r
nd yo

alpha
books

A Division of Prentice Hall Computer Publishing
11711 North College Avenue, Carmel, Indiana 46032 USA

Dedication

To my sister Pat, who introduced me to WordPerfect and remains one of its loyal fans.

Acknowledgments

Special thanks to Seta Frantz for helping me with the vision of this book, and Lisa Bucki for allowing me to write it—I had fun! Also, loving thanks to Scott, who understands me better than I do myself.

International Standard Book Number: 1-56761-177-x
Library of Congress Catalog Card Number: 93-70253

95 94 93   9 8 7 6 5 4 3 2 1

Interpretation of the printing code: the rightmost number of the first series of numbers is the year of the book's printing; the rightmost number of the second series of numbers is the number of the book's printing. For example, a printing code of 93-1 shows that the first printing of the book occurred in 1993.

Screen reproductions in this book were created by means of the program Collage Plus from Inner Media, Inc., Hollis, NH.

Printed in the United States of America by
Shepard Poorman Communications Corp.
7301 N. Woodland Drive, Indianapolis, IN 46278

TRADEMARKS

Publisher

Marie Butler-Knight

Associate Publisher

Lisa A. Bucki

Managing Editor

Elizabeth Keaffaber

Acquisitions Manager

Stephen R. Poland

Manuscript Editor

San Dee Phillips

Cover Designer

Scott Fullmer

Designer

Amy Peppler-Adams

Indexer

Jeanne Clark

Production Team

*Diana Bigham, Katy Bodenmiller, Scott Cook, Tim Cox,
Linda Koopman, Tom Loveman, Beth Rago, Carrie Roth, Greg Simsic*

*Special thanks to Kelly Oliver for ensuring the
technical accuracy of this book.*

CONTENTS

Part 4 Changing the Way Your Document Looks **93**

Part 5 Features That Make Life Easier **119**

Glossary **131**

Installing WordPerfect 6 **135**

Index **137**

INTRODUCTION

Have you ever said to yourself, "I wish someone would just *show me* how to use WordPerfect?" If you have, this Show Me book is for you. In it, you won't find detailed explanations of what's going on in your computer each time you enter a command. Instead, you will see pictures that *show you*, step-by-step, how to perform a particular task.

This book will make you feel as though you have your very own personal trainer standing next to you, pointing at the screen, and showing you exactly how to use WordPerfect.

WHAT IS WORDPERFECT?

WordPerfect is a *word processor*. A word processor is a typewriter for your computer. Using a word processor, you can type text and then make changes to it. When you insert or delete text, WordPerfect adjusts your words automatically so everything stays within the margins (and there are no gaping holes left by deleted words).

Using a word processor such as WordPerfect, you can easily:

- Check for spelling and grammatical errors before you print.
- Center titles and headings, or add bold or italic lettering to make them stand out.
- Print out as many copies as you want.
- Save your work so that next month you can change a report or a memo without having to completely retype it.

A Day in the Life of a Word Processor

What you create with a word processor is called a *document*. So whether you use WordPerfect to create a letter, a report, or a memo, you are creating *individual documents*. You can save documents, print documents, and edit (change) documents. As you create your document in WordPerfect, you follow a basic pattern:

Open an existing document, or create a new one. You start your work session by typing text into a new document or by editing an existing one.

Type in some text. This part is easy; just type!

Read what you've written and make changes. At this stage, you're copying or moving text from one place to another. You may even delete some text or insert new text to clarify a point. The process of making changes to existing text is called *editing*.

Add pizzazz. Changing the way characters look (such as adding bold or making characters bigger) is called *formatting*.

Spell check your document. WordPerfect comes with a spell checker which checks your words. You can also use the grammar checker to look for errors in context. Of course, nothing can replace the actual process of re-reading your text for sense, but these powerful tools help ensure that your documents look professional.

Save your document. Once you're sure you have a document that you like, you should save it. Actually, it's best to save a document often during the editing phase so you can't lose any changes.

View your document before you print it. WordPerfect gives you many ways to view your text—as you are working and right before you print your document.

Print your document. Nothing is better than holding the finished product in your own hands.

The Odds and Ends of Using a Word Processor

Before you begin to use a word processor, you need to understand a few things:

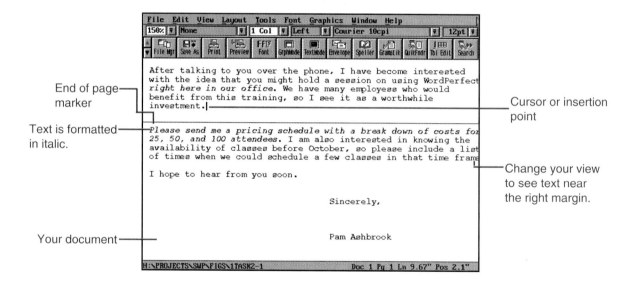

The cursor marks the place where text will be inserted. To insert text within a paragraph, you move the cursor (a blinking vertical line) to the point where you want to begin, and then you type.

What you see isn't necessarily what you get. The right-hand margin that you see on your screen may not be the right-hand margin of your document. WordPerfect provides several ways for you to view your document on-screen; in one mode, the text is large and comfortable to work with—but you may not see the right-hand margin of your document when you work in that mode.

A solid line marks the end of a page. Just cross over the solid line when you see it; a solid line tells WordPerfect where one page ends and another begins. If you add text above a solid line, the excess text at the bottom of that page will flow onto the next page automatically.

Formatting describes the way something looks. Character *formatting* describes how a character looks. (For example, is it **bold** or *italic*?) Paragraph formatting describes the alignment of a paragraph. (For example, is it centered?) To save time, you can save the formatting of a paragraph as a *style*, and reapply that same formatting to many paragraphs with a few keystrokes.

HOW TO USE THIS BOOK

Using this book is as simple as falling off your chair. Just flip to the task that you want to perform and follow the steps. You will see easy step-by-step instructions that tell you which keys to press and which commands to select. You will also see step-by-step pictures that show you what to do. Follow the steps or the pictures (or both) to complete the task.

Saving a Document and Continuing to Work

1 Click on the **File** menu or press **Alt+F**.

2 Click on Save **As**, or press **A**.

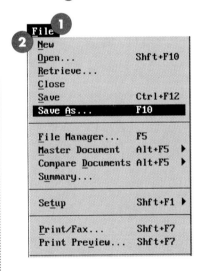

3 If this is the first time you've saved this document, or if you want to save this document under a new name, enter a name for the file.

4 Click on **OK**, or press **Enter** to save the file.

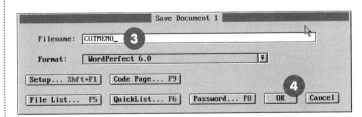

Every computer book has its own way of telling you which buttons to push and which keys to press. Here's how this book handles those formalities:

- Keys that you should press appear as they do on your keyboard; for example, press **Alt** or press **F10**. If you need to press more than one key at once, the keys are separated with plus signs. For example, if the text tells you to press **Alt+F**, hold down the **Alt** key while pressing the **F** key.

- Text that you should type is printed in **boldface type like this**.

- Some commands are activated by selecting a menu and then a command. If I tell you to "select **File New**," you should open the **File** menu and select the **New** command. In this book, the *selection letter* is printed in boldface for easy recognition.

LEARNING THE LINGO

Selection letter: A single letter of a menu command, such as the *x* in E**x**it, which activates the command when the menu is open and that letter is pressed.

Definitions in Plain English

In addition to the basic step-by-step approach, pages may contain Learning the Lingo definitions to help you understand key terms. These definitions are placed off to the side, so you can easily skip them.

LEARNING THE LINGO

Pull-down menu: A menu that appears at the top of the screen, listing various options. The menu is not visible until you select it from the menu bar. The menu then drops down, covering a small part of the screen.

Quick Refreshers

If you need to know how to perform some other task in order to perform the current task, look for a Quick Refresher. With the Quick Refresher, you won't have to flip through the book to learn how to perform the other task; the information is right where you need it.

QUICK REFRESHER

Making dialog box selections

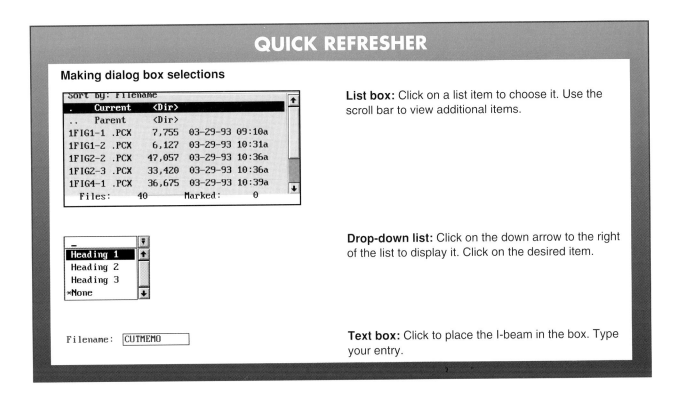

List box: Click on a list item to choose it. Use the scroll bar to view additional items.

Drop-down list: Click on the down arrow to the right of the list to display it. Click on the desired item.

Text box: Click to place the I-beam in the box. Type your entry.

Tips, Ideas, and Shortcuts

Throughout this book, you will encounter tips that provide important information about a task or that tell you how to perform the task more quickly.

TIP

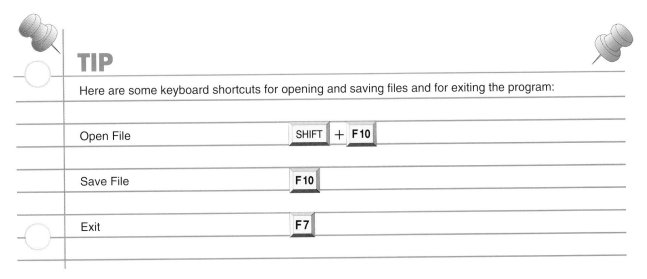

Here are some keyboard shortcuts for opening and saving files and for exiting the program:

Open File   SHIFT + F10

Save File   F10

Exit   F7

Exercises

Because most people learn by doing, exercises throughout the book give you additional practice performing a task.

Exercise

Practice what you've learned about using menus by switching the view:

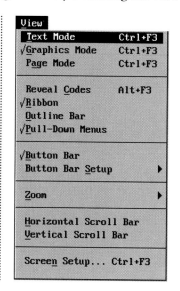

1 Open the View menu by clicking on it or by pressing **Alt+V**.

2 Select **Text** Mode by clicking on it or by pressing **T**.

3 Open the View menu again by clicking on it or by pressing **Alt+V**.

4 Select the **Graphics** Mode command by clicking on it or by pressing **G**.

Where Should You Start?

If this is your first encounter with computers, read the next section, "Quick Computer Tour," before reading anything else. This section explains some computer basics that you need to know in order to get your computer up and running.

Once you know the basics, you can work through this book from beginning to end or skip around from task to task, as needed. If you decide to skip around, there are several ways you can find what you're looking for:

- Use the Table of Contents at the front of this book to find a specific task you want to perform.

- Use the complete index at the back of this book to look up a specific task or topic and find the page number on which it is covered.

- Use the color-coded sections to find groups of related tasks.

- Flip through the book, and look at the task titles at the top of the pages. This method works best if you know the general location of the task in the book.

- Use the inside back cover of this book to quickly find the page where a command you are looking for is covered.

QUICK COMPUTER TOUR

If this is your first time in front of a computer, the next few sections will teach you the least you need to know to get started.

Parts of a Computer

Think of a computer as a car. The system unit holds the engine that powers the computer. The monitor is like the windshield that lets you see where you're going. And the keyboard and mouse are like the steering wheel, which allow you to control the computer.

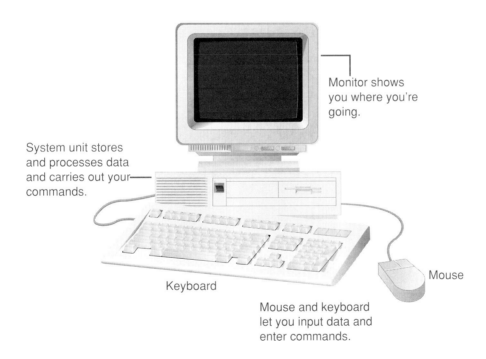

Monitor shows you where you're going.

System unit stores and processes data and carries out your commands.

Keyboard

Mouse

Mouse and keyboard let you input data and enter commands.

The System Unit

The system unit contains three basic elements: a central processing unit (CPU) that does all the "thinking" for the computer; random-access memory (RAM) that stores instructions and data while the CPU is processing it; and disk drives, which store information permanently on disks to keep the information safe. It also contains several ports (at the back), which allow you to connect other devices to it, such as a keyboard, mouse, and printer.

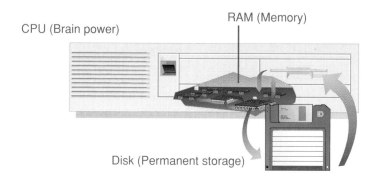

CPU (Brain power)

RAM (Memory)

Disk (Permanent storage)

Using a Keyboard

The keyboard is no mystery. It contains a set of alphanumeric (letter and number) keys for entering text, arrow keys for moving around on-screen, and function keys (F1, F2, and so on) for entering commands. It also has some odd keys, including Alt (Alternative), Ctrl (Control), and Esc (Escape) that perform special actions.

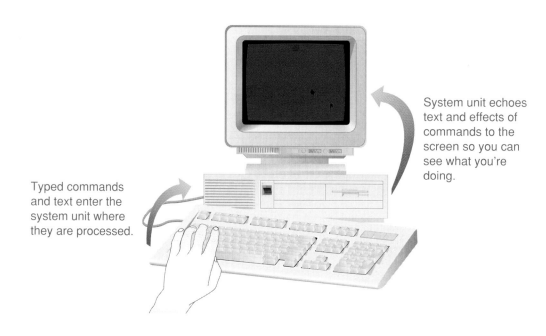

System unit echoes text and effects of commands to the screen so you can see what you're doing.

Typed commands and text enter the system unit where they are processed.

Using a Mouse

Like the keyboard, a mouse allows you to communicate with the computer. You roll the mouse around on your desk to move a *mouse pointer* on the screen. You can use the pointer to open menus and select other items on-screen. Here are some mouse techniques you must master:

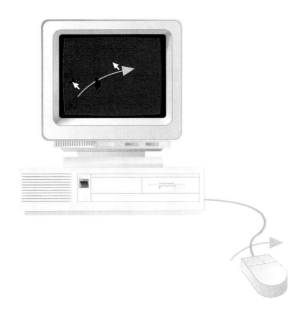

Pointing. To point, roll the mouse on your desk until the tip of the mouse pointer is on the item you want to point to.

Clicking. To click on an item, point to the desired item, and then hold the mouse steady while you press and release the mouse button. Use the left mouse button unless I tell you specifically to use the right button.

Double-clicking. To double-click, hold the mouse steady while you press and release the mouse button twice quickly.

Right-clicking. To right-click, click using the right mouse button instead of the left button.

Understanding Disks, Directories, and Files

Whatever you type (a letter, a list of names, a tax return) is stored only in your computer's temporary memory and is erased when the electricity is turned off. To protect your work, you must save it in a *file* on a *disk*.

A *file* is like a folder that you might use to store a report or a letter. You name the file, so you can later find and retrieve the information it contains.

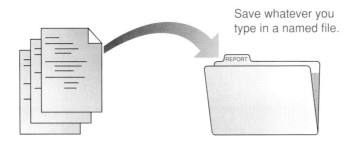

Save whatever you type in a named file.

Files are stored on *disks*. Your computer probably has a *hard disk* inside it (called drive C) to which you can save your files. You can also save files to *floppy disks*, which you insert into the slots (the floppy disk drives) on the front of the computer.

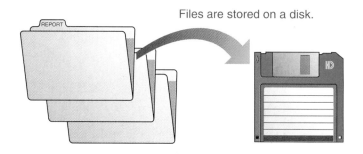

Files are stored on a disk.

To keep files organized on a disk, you can create *directories* on the disk. Each directory acts as a drawer in a filing cabinet, storing a group of related files. Although you can create directories on both floppy and hard disks, most people use directories only on hard disks.

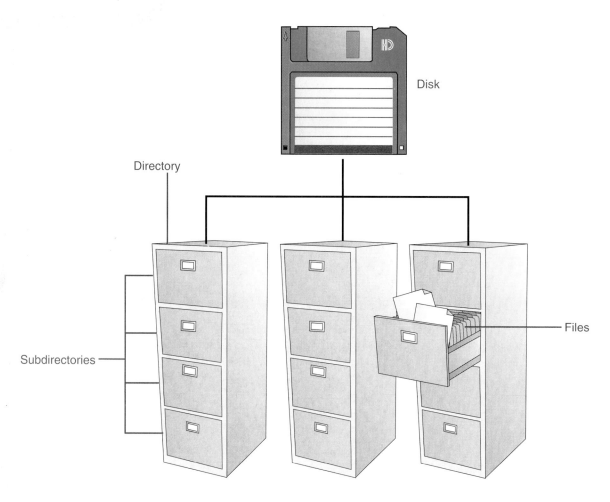

Disk

Directory

Subdirectories

Files

PART 1

Basic WordPerfect Tasks

In this part, you will learn the essentials for using WordPerfect. You'll learn how to start WordPerfect, move around the screen, issue commands, and, of course, how to exit. Here's a list of the tasks in this part:

- Starting WordPerfect
- Changing Viewing Modes
- Selecting a Menu Command
- Using Dialog Boxes
- Displaying and Using the Button Bar
- Moving the Button Bar
- Getting Help from WordPerfect
- Exiting WordPerfect

STARTING WORDPERFECT

How Do I Start WordPerfect?

Before you can use WordPerfect to create or edit *documents*, you must first start (load) it at the DOS prompt. As WordPerfect is starting, you'll see a message displaying the version number of the program and then the program's main screen. The most current version is 6.0, and that is the version whose screens you will see in this book.

Pull down a menu from the menu bar to select a command.

The insertion point or cursor marks your place within the text.

Move the mouse pointer to select text or choose commands.

Enter your text into the text area.

The Status Line displays information about your location within the document.

LEARNING THE LINGO

Document: Any work you create using a word processor, such as a letter or a memo.

Directory: Because large hard disks can store thousands of files, you often need to store related files in separate directories on the disk. Think of your disk as a filing cabinet and think of each directory as a drawer in the filing cabinet. By keeping files in separate directories, you can easily locate and work with related files.

DOS prompt: An on-screen prompt that indicates DOS is ready to accept a command. The DOS prompt looks something like **C>** or **C:\>**.

Starting WordPerfect

1 At the *DOS prompt* (**C:\>**), type **CD\WP60**.

```
C:\>CD\WP60  1
```

2 Press **Enter** to change to the WordPerfect *directory*.

ENTER **2**

3 At the DOS prompt, type **WP**.

```
C:\>CD\WP60

C:\WP60>WP  3
```

4 Press **Enter**.

ENTER **4**

TIP

When you start WordPerfect, it starts in Text Mode. You can switch to Graphics Mode using the "Changing Viewing Modes" task in this part.

Basic WordPerfect Tasks

CHANGING VIEWING MODES

Why Change Your View?

When you start WordPerfect, it starts in *Text Mode*. There is another viewing mode that you can use called *Graphics Mode*. Optional screen parts, such as the *Ribbon* and the *Button Bar*, display very differently in Text Mode than in Graphics Mode. You'll probably want to work in Graphics Mode all the time because the parts of the Ribbon and the Button Bar are easier to identify and therefore, easier to use.

By the way, the Ribbon and the Button Bar will not display until you "turn them on." To learn how to display them, see the "Displaying and Using the Button Bar" task later in this part and the "Displaying and Using the Ribbon" task in Part IV.

This is how the Ribbon looks in Text Mode.

Here's how your mouse pointer looks in Text Mode.

Bold displays as white letters.

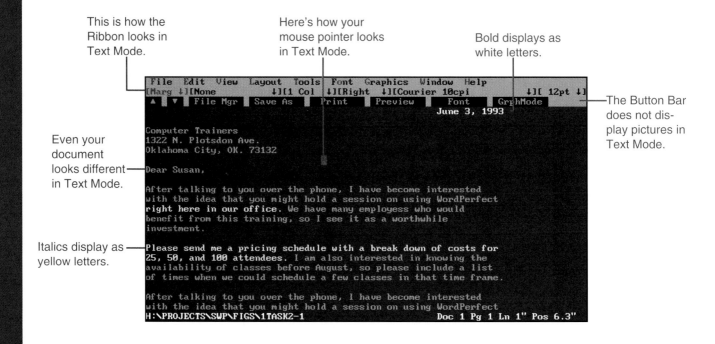

Even your document looks different in Text Mode.

Italics display as yellow letters.

The Button Bar does not display pictures in Text Mode.

LEARNING THE LINGO

Ribbon: Optionally displays at the top of the WordPerfect screen, just under the menu bar. The Ribbon provides quick access to commands that change the way your text is displayed.

Button Bar: Optionally displays at the top of the WordPerfect screen, just under the Ribbon. The Button Bar provides quick access to the most often used commands, such as saving a document.

The Ribbon looks slightly different in Graphics Mode.

The mouse pointer really "points" in Graphics Mode.

Italics and other character formatting display as they will print.

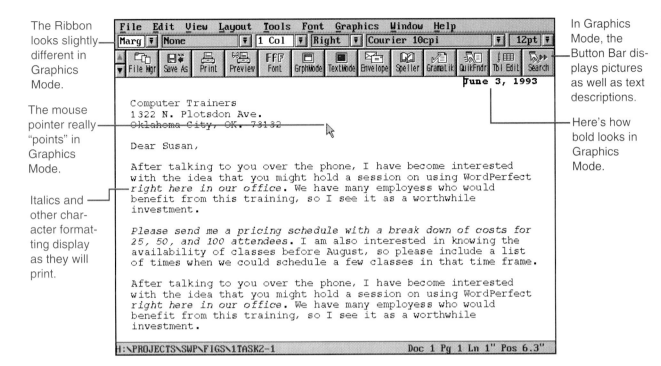

In Graphics Mode, the Button Bar displays pictures as well as text descriptions.

Here's how bold looks in Graphics Mode.

When you open the **V**iew menu, the current viewing mode is marked with either an asterisk (if you're currently in Text Mode) or a check mark (if you're in Graphics Mode).

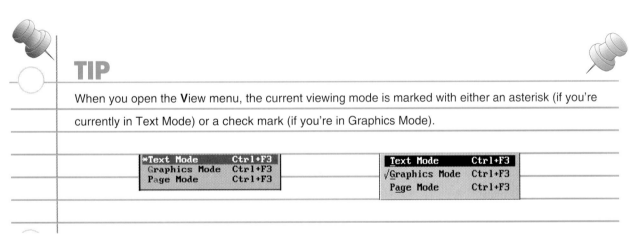

CHANGING VIEWING MODES

Changing to Graphics Mode

1 Open the **View** menu by clicking on it or pressing **Alt+V**.

2 Click on **Graphics Mode**, or press **G**.

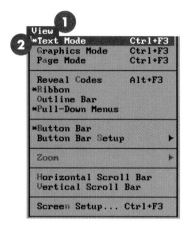

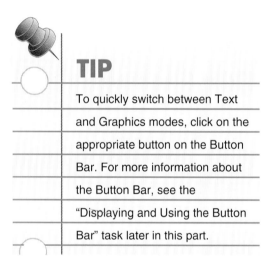

TIP

To quickly switch between Text and Graphics modes, click on the appropriate button on the Button Bar. For more information about the Button Bar, see the "Displaying and Using the Button Bar" task later in this part.

QUICK REFRESHER

Click: To click, you move the mouse pointer so that it rests on top of the item you want to select, then press the left mouse button.

SELECTING A MENU COMMAND

What Is a Menu Command?

Tucked away at the top of the WordPerfect screen, you'll see something called a menu bar. The menu bar is like a salad bar, except instead of choosing from carrots, mushrooms, and radishes, you're choosing commands.

The menu bar lists the main menus, such as **File**, **Edit**, **View**, and so on. Under each of these menus, there are additional selections called *commands*, but you can't see them until you *pull down* (open) the menu. Each of the WordPerfect pull-down menus provides a set of commands for a specific purpose. For example, the **File** menu provides commands that you can use to create, save, and print your *files* (among other things). You'll learn the specific purpose of each menu as we go on.

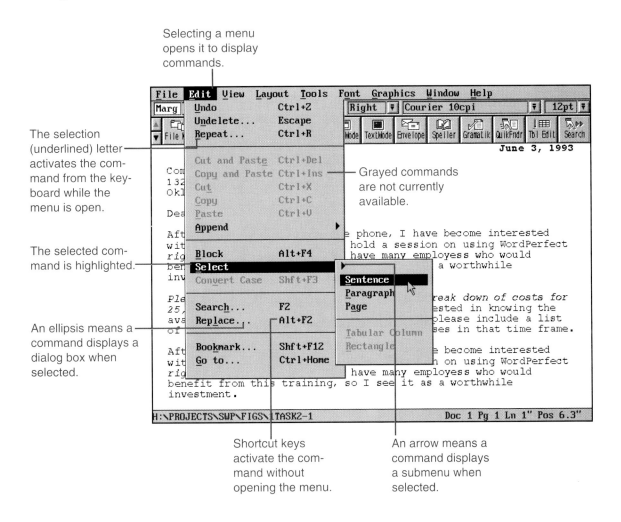

Selecting a menu opens it to display commands.

The selection (underlined) letter activates the command from the keyboard while the menu is open.

The selected command is highlighted.

An ellipsis means a command displays a dialog box when selected.

Grayed commands are not currently available.

Shortcut keys activate the command without opening the menu.

An arrow means a command displays a submenu when selected.

17

SELECTING A MENU COMMAND

Selecting a Menu Command

1 To open a pull-down menu, click on the menu name. To open a pull-down menu with the keyboard, press and hold down the **Alt** key as you press the key corresponding to the underlined letter in the menu name.

2 To select a command from the open menu, click on the command. To select a command with the keyboard, press the selection letter (the underlined letter in the command).

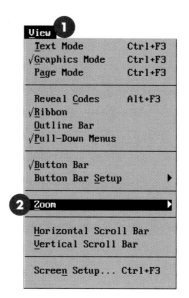

```
View ①
   Text Mode          Ctrl+F3
 √Graphics Mode       Ctrl+F3
   Page Mode          Ctrl+F3

   Reveal Codes       Alt+F3
 √Ribbon
   Outline Bar
 √Pull-Down Menus

 √Button Bar
   Button Bar Setup            ▶

② Zoom                         ▶

   Horizontal Scroll Bar
   Vertical Scroll Bar

   Screen Setup... Ctrl+F3
```

3 If a submenu is displayed, click on the command you want to select, or press the selection letter (the underlined letter).

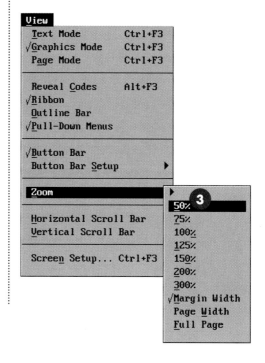

```
View
   Text Mode          Ctrl+F3
 √Graphics Mode       Ctrl+F3
   Page Mode          Ctrl+F3

   Reveal Codes       Alt+F3
 √Ribbon
   Outline Bar
 √Pull-Down Menus

 √Button Bar
   Button Bar Setup            ▶

   Zoom                        ▶   ③
                                 50%
   Horizontal Scroll Bar         75%
   Vertical Scroll Bar           100%
                                 125%
   Screen Setup... Ctrl+F3       150%
                                 200%
                                 300%
                               √Margin Width
                                 Page Width
                                 Full Page
```

TIP

You can also select commands from an open menu by using the up or down arrow keys to highlight the command and then pressing **Enter**.

TIP

To close a menu you opened by accident, press **Esc** or click anywhere in the document.

QUICK REFRESHER

You can select a command with the keyboard *without* opening the menu by using its *shortcut key*. If a shortcut key consists of two keys, such as Ctrl+F3, press and hold the first key (in this case, **Ctrl**), and then press the second key (in this case, **F3**).

```
 Text Mode      Ctrl+F3
√Graphics Mode  Ctrl+F3
 Page Mode      Ctrl+F3
```

Selection letters are underlined on WordPerfect menus, but they appear as bold letters in this book, as in **T**ext Mode.

```
View
 Text Mode      Ctrl+F3
√Graphics Mode  Ctrl+F3
 Page Mode      Ctrl+F3
```

Some commands, such as the Ribbon command, are turned "on" when you select them the first time, and "off" when you select them again. These commands are marked with a check mark or an asterisk when they are "on."

```
 Reveal Codes   Alt+F3
√Ribbon
 Outline Bar
√Pull-Down Menus
```

LEARNING THE LINGO

Pull-down menu: A pull-down menu contains commands you can select. Activating this type of menu pulls it down below the main menu bar, like a window shade can be pulled down from the top of a window frame.

File: DOS stores information in files. Anything can be placed in a file: a memo, a budget report, or even a graphics image (such as a picture of a person or a computer). Each document you create in WordPerfect is stored in its own file. Files always have a file name to identify them.

Dialog box: A dialog box is a special window that appears when WordPerfect requires additional information before a command can be executed.

Basic WordPerfect Tasks

USING DIALOG BOXES

What Is a Dialog Box?

When you select a menu command followed by an ellipsis, as in the **Edit Search**... command, a dialog box appears. A dialog box is a special window that appears when WordPerfect requires additional information before a command can be executed. Dialog boxes are made up of individual elements with each serving a specific function.

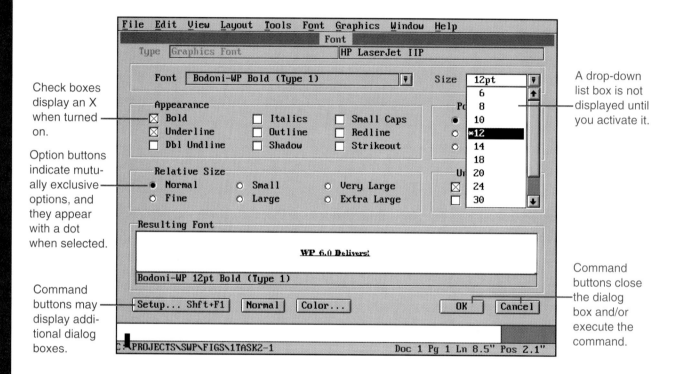

Check boxes display an X when turned on.

Option buttons indicate mutually exclusive options, and they appear with a dot when selected.

Command buttons may display additional dialog boxes.

A drop-down list box is not displayed until you activate it.

Command buttons close the dialog box and/or execute the command.

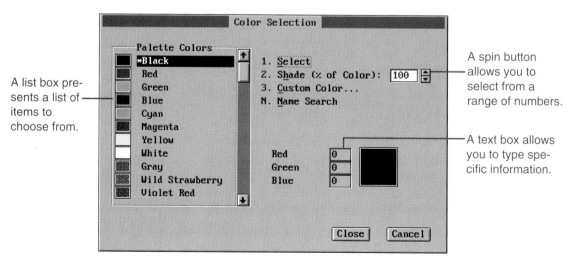

A list box presents a list of items to choose from.

A spin button allows you to select from a range of numbers.

A text box allows you to type specific information.

Selecting the Various Options Within a Dialog Box

To move around a dialog box, click on any item to activate it, or press **Tab** to move to an area. Then press **Enter** to activate it. (On most screens, the active area of the dialog box will display with a blue ring around it.)

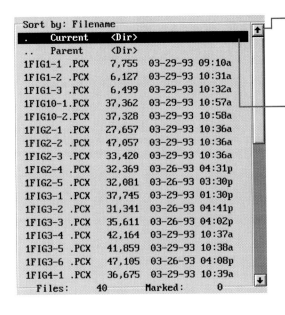

If a list has a scroll bar, click on the arrows at the top or bottom of the scroll bar to move through the list. To move through a list quickly, click on the scroll bar between the arrows.

To select an item from a list box, click on a list item to choose it. Use the scroll bar to view additional items.

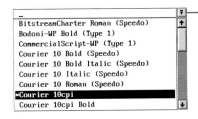

To select an item from a drop-down list, click on the down arrow to the right of the list, and then click on the desired item to select it. With the keyboard, press **Tab** until the area is highlighted, and then press **Enter** to display the list items. Use the arrow keys to highlight an item, and press **Enter**.

To select a check box, click on a box to select or deselect it. If you use the keyboard, press **Tab** until the area is highlighted, then press **Enter**. Press the underlined letter of the check box you want to select. (You can select more than one.)

continues

Basic WordPerfect Tasks

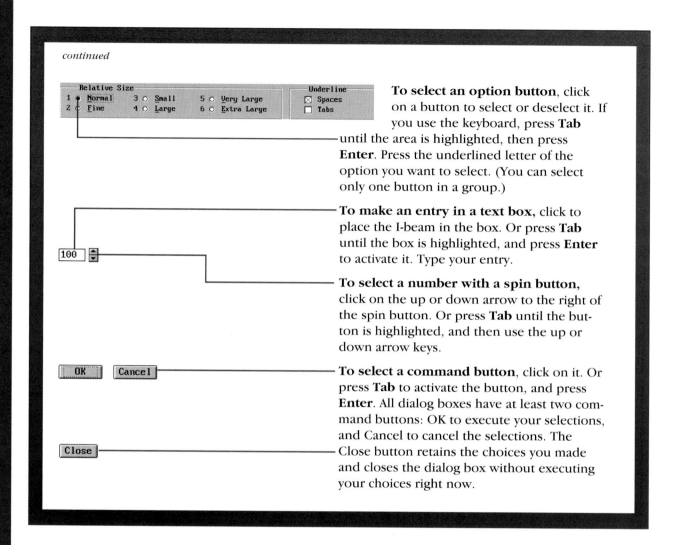

continued

To select an option button, click on a button to select or deselect it. If you use the keyboard, press **Tab** until the area is highlighted, then press **Enter**. Press the underlined letter of the option you want to select. (You can select only one button in a group.)

To make an entry in a text box, click to place the I-beam in the box. Or press **Tab** until the box is highlighted, and press **Enter** to activate it. Type your entry.

To select a number with a spin button, click on the up or down arrow to the right of the spin button. Or press **Tab** until the button is highlighted, and then use the up or down arrow keys.

To select a command button, click on it. Or press **Tab** to activate the button, and press **Enter**. All dialog boxes have at least two command buttons: OK to execute your selections, and Cancel to cancel the selections. The Close button retains the choices you made and closes the dialog box without executing your choices right now.

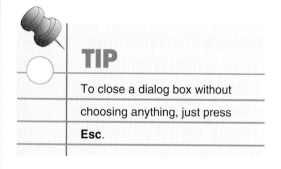

TIP

To close a dialog box without choosing anything, just press **Esc**.

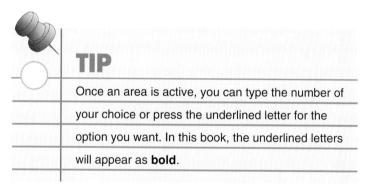

TIP

Once an area is active, you can type the number of your choice or press the underlined letter for the option you want. In this book, the underlined letters will appear as **bold**.

DISPLAYING AND USING THE BUTTON BAR

Why Use the Button Bar?

If you use a mouse, the Button Bar is the quickest way for you to select the most common commands. (Sorry, you can't use the Button Bar with the keyboard.) When you start WordPerfect for the first time, the Button Bar is not displayed. When you "turn it on," the Button Bar is displayed at the top of the WordPerfect screen, just below the *Ribbon* (if it is "on"). The little squares that make up the Button Bar are called *buttons* because you "press" them (click on them with the mouse) to select them. They are also called *icons* because they contain little pictures that represent the task they perform. Actually, some of those icons are a bit obscure, so here's a rundown of the function of each button.

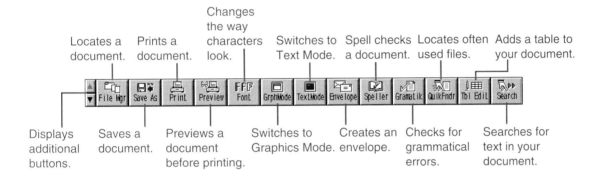

Locates a document. — Prints a document. — Changes the way characters look. — Switches to Text Mode. — Spell checks a document. — Locates often used files. — Adds a table to your document.

Displays additional buttons. — Saves a document. — Previews a document before printing. — Switches to Graphics Mode. — Creates an envelope. — Checks for grammatical errors. — Searches for text in your document.

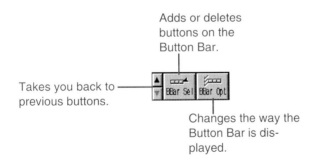

Adds or deletes buttons on the Button Bar.

Takes you back to previous buttons.

Changes the way the Button Bar is displayed.

DISPLAYING AND USING THE BUTTON BAR

Displaying and Using the Button Bar

1 Click on the **V**iew menu, or press **Alt+V**.

2 Click on **B**utton Bar, or press **B**.

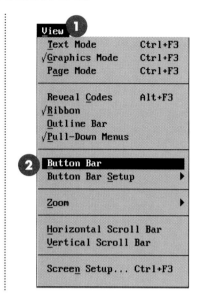

LEARNING THE LINGO

Ribbon: Optionally displays at the top of the WordPerfect screen, just under the menu bar. The Ribbon provides quick access to commands that change the way your text is displayed.

Icon: A graphic image that represents a command.

TIP

To use a button, click on it.

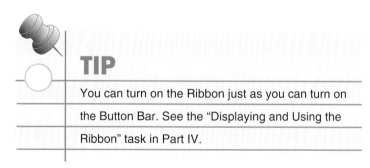

TIP

You can turn on the Ribbon just as you can turn on the Button Bar. See the "Displaying and Using the Ribbon" task in Part IV.

MOVING THE BUTTON BAR

Why Move the Button Bar?

The Button Bar is normally displayed at the top of the WordPerfect screen, just under the Ribbon (if the Ribbon is displayed). If you like, you can choose to display the Button Bar on the left, right or even the bottom of the screen. You can also elect to display just pictures or just text within the buttons of the Button Bar.

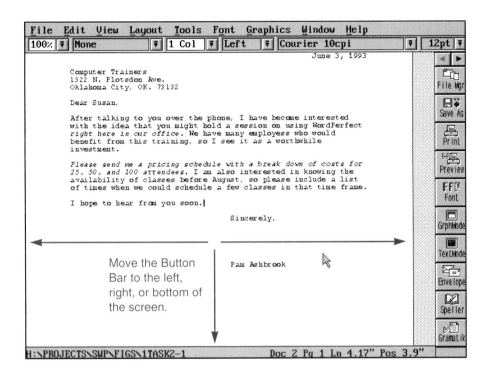

Move the Button Bar to the left, right, or bottom of the screen.

Normally, both text and pictures are displayed within each button.

After you are familiar with the purpose of each tool, you may want to display only pictures within each button.

Or if you prefer, display only text.

25

Moving the Button Bar

1 Click on the **View** menu, or press **Alt+V**.

2 Click on Button Bar Setup, or press **S**.

3 Click on **Options**, or press **O**.

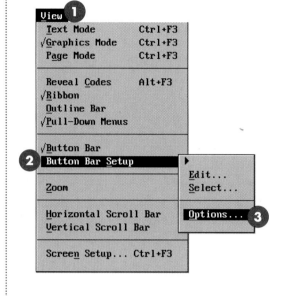

4 Select a position for the Button Bar.

5 Choose between **P**icture and Text, Picture **O**nly, or Te**x**t Only.

6 Click **OK** or press **Enter**.

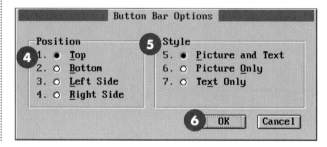

TIP

Use the Button Bar Options button to change the position of the Button Bar or what it displays: text, pictures or text and pictures.

GETTING HELP FROM WORDPERFECT

When Can You Get Help?

Help in WordPerfect is *context-sensitive*, which means that Help knows what you're doing. When you access Help, it takes you to a part that explains that specific task. For example, when you use the command to save a document, a dialog box appears, asking for more information (such as a name for the file). If you don't know what to do when the dialog box appears, just access Help, and you'll be taken to the part in the help system that talks about saving your document.

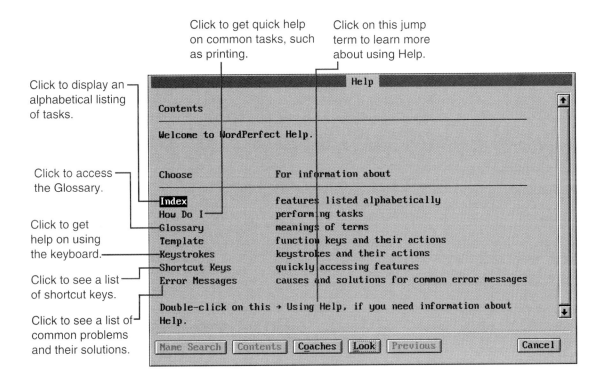

Click to get quick help on common tasks, such as printing.

Click on this jump term to learn more about using Help.

Click to display an alphabetical listing of tasks.

Click to access the Glossary.

Click to get help on using the keyboard.

Click to see a list of shortcut keys.

Click to see a list of common problems and their solutions.

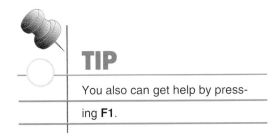

TIP

You also can get help by pressing **F1**.

LEARNING THE LINGO

Glossary: A section of the WordPerfect help system where you can find definitions of terms.

Jump term: A highlighted term that when selected, "jumps" you to a related section of the help system.

Basic WordPerfect Tasks

GETTING HELP FROM WORDPERFECT

Getting Help

1 Click on the **Help** menu, or press **Alt+H**.

2 Click on Contents, or press **C**.

3 Click on a Help category or use the up or down arrow keys to highlight a category, and press **Enter**.

4 Click on **Name Search** to search for instructions for a specific task, or press **N**.

5 Click on Contents to return to this screen, or press **C**.

6 Click on Coaches to have one of the WordPerfect coaches help you complete a specific task, or press **O**.

7 Click on **Look** or press **L** to look up a selected glossary or jump term.

8 Click on **Previous** to move to the previous screen in the help system, or press **P**.

9 Click on **Cancel** or press **Esc** to exit the Help system.

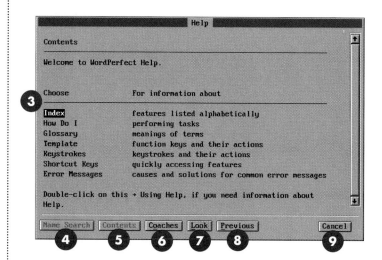

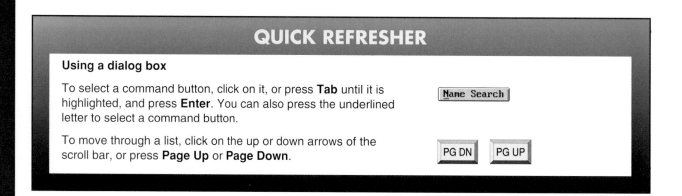

QUICK REFRESHER

Using a dialog box

To select a command button, click on it, or press **Tab** until it is highlighted, and press **Enter**. You can also press the underlined letter to select a command button.

To move through a list, click on the up or down arrows of the scroll bar, or press **Page Up** or **Page Down**.

Exercise

Follow these steps to practice moving around the WordPerfect help system.

1 Press **F1**.

2 Double-click on **Index**, or press **Enter**.

3 Click on **Name Search**, or press **N**.

4 Type **Exit**, and press **Enter**. (This searches for Exit in the index.)

5 Double-click on **Exit**, or press **Enter** to get help on exiting WordPerfect.

6 Read the steps. Double-click on any jump term to move to another section of help.

7 Press **Esc**, or click on **Cancel**.

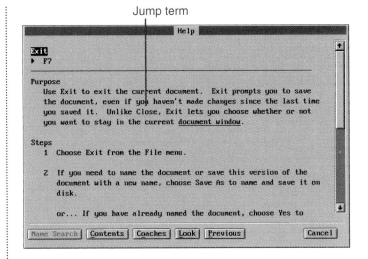

Jump term

```
                          Help
Exit
▶ F7

Purpose
  Use Exit to exit the current document.  Exit prompts you to save
  the document, even if you haven't made changes since the last time
  you saved it.  Unlike Close, Exit lets you choose whether or not
  you want to stay in the current document window.

Steps
  1  Choose Exit from the File menu.

  2  If you need to name the document or save this version of the
     document with a new name, choose Save As to name and save it on
     disk.

     or... If you have already named the document, choose Yes to

 Name Search   Contents   Coaches   Look   Previous          Cancel
```

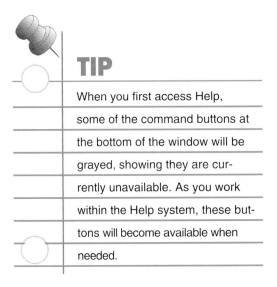

TIP

When you first access Help, some of the command buttons at the bottom of the window will be grayed, showing they are currently unavailable. As you work within the Help system, these buttons will become available when needed.

TIP

WordPerfect includes two additional help sources: *tutorials* and *coaches*. A tutorial consists of a series of tasks within a single lesson. The most popular WordPerfect tasks are presented here in a hands-on style that lets you practice the commands without affecting your document.

When you're playing on a team, a coach gives you guidelines on what to do and when. The WordPerfect coaches are similar; they guide you through changes to your document step by step.

Access either the tutorials or the coaches through the Help menu.

Basic WordPerfect Tasks

EXITING WORDPERFECT

When Can I Exit WordPerfect?

You can exit WordPerfect at any time, but before you do, you should save your documents. If you don't save your documents before you exit, your changes will be lost. When you exit WordPerfect, you will get either one of two dialog boxes: if you've saved your document at least once during the work session, you'll get the Exit dialog box. If you've never saved your document, you'll get a similar dialog box that includes a Save and Exit button instead. You should try to save your documents often throughout a work session. See the tasks on saving documents in Part III.

Exiting WordPerfect

1 Click on the **File** menu, or press **Alt+F**.

2 Click on **Exit WP**, or press **X**.

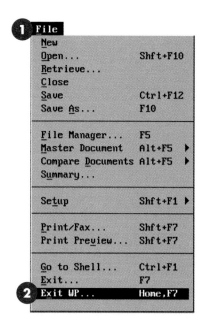

3 Click on **Save and Exit** or **Exit**, or press **Enter**.

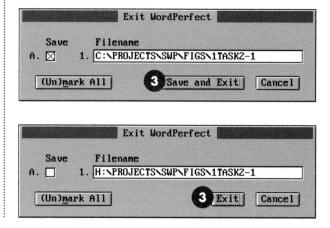

PART 2

Creating and Editing Documents

In this part, you will learn the skills you'll need to "get down to work" creating and editing your documents. You'll use the skills you learn next over and over again as you create letters, memos, and reports.

- Typing Text
- Zooming In and Out
- Correcting Text
- Selecting a Sentence, Paragraph, or Page
- Selecting Blocks of Text
- Deleting Selected Text
- Undeleting Text
- Inserting a Date
- Copying and Moving Text
- Starting a New Page
- Searching for Text
- Replacing Text

TYPING TEXT

How Do You Type Text?

When you start WordPerfect, the *cursor* (or insertion point) is automatically placed at the top of an empty document window so that you are ready to start entering text. As you type, your words will automatically advance to the next line at the appropriate point. This is called *word wrapping.* If you insert words into the middle of a paragraph, the rest of the paragraph will be automatically adjusted. Press Enter *only when you reach the end of a paragraph or to insert a blank line.*

If you want to divide an existing paragraph in two, move the cursor to the dividing point and press **Enter**. If you forget and press **Enter** at the end of a line, you'll create two paragraphs. To join two paragraphs together, move to the first letter of the second paragraph and press **Backspace**.

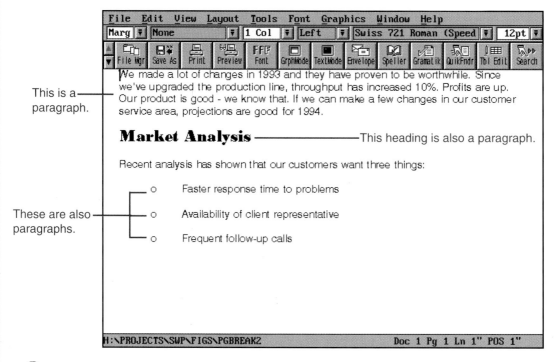

This is a paragraph.

We made a lot of changes in 1993 and they have proven to be worthwhile. Since we've upgraded the production line, throughput has increased 10%. Profits are up. Our product is good - we know that. If we can make a few changes in our customer service area, projections are good for 1994.

Market Analysis ————————— This heading is also a paragraph.

Recent analysis has shown that our customers want three things:

These are also paragraphs.

   o   Faster response time to problems

   o   Availability of client representative

   o   Frequent follow-up calls

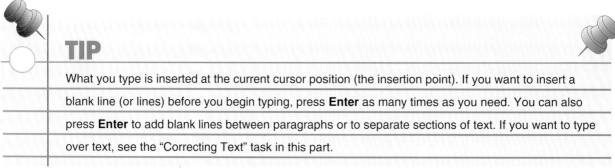

TIP

What you type is inserted at the current cursor position (the insertion point). If you want to insert a blank line (or lines) before you begin typing, press **Enter** as many times as you need. You can also press **Enter** to add blank lines between paragraphs or to separate sections of text. If you want to type over text, see the "Correcting Text" task in this part.

Typing Text

1 Move the cursor to the point where you'd like to insert text.

2 Type your text.

3 When you come to the end of a paragraph, press **Enter**.

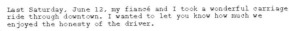

Last Saturday, June 12, my fiancé and I took a wonderful carriage ride through downtown. I wanted to let you know how much we enjoyed the honesty of the driver.

1 **2** After finishing our ride, I noticed that I had left my purse on the seat of the carriage. We looked around and the driver had already left. When he returned, the driver noticed me and pulled out my purse from under his seat, where he had been keeping it safe. **3**

Please thank him for me (I think his name was Tom).

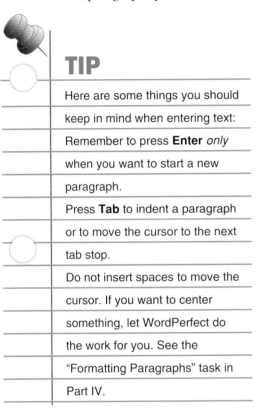

TIP

Here are some things you should keep in mind when entering text:

Remember to press **Enter** *only* when you want to start a new paragraph.

Press **Tab** to indent a paragraph or to move the cursor to the next tab stop.

Do not insert spaces to move the cursor. If you want to center something, let WordPerfect do the work for you. See the "Formatting Paragraphs" task in Part IV.

LEARNING THE LINGO

Cursor: A vertical blinking line that moves across the page as you type. A cursor acts like the tip of your pencil; anything you type appears at the cursor. Also called *insertion point*.

Word wrapping: With word wrapping, words you type are automatically advanced to the next line of a paragraph when they "bump" into the right-hand margin. If you change the margins, paragraphs adjust automatically.

Paragraph: Any grouping of words that should be treated as a unit. This includes normal paragraphs, as well as single line paragraphs, such as chapter titles, section headings, and captions for charts or other figures. Pressing Enter marks the end of a paragraph.

Creating and Editing Documents

TYPING TEXT

Exercise

Follow the steps in this exercise to practice entering text. If you make a mistake while typing, press **Backspace** until you erase the mistake, and then retype it. (See the "Correcting Text" task later in this part for more tips on how to correct mistakes.)

1 Type **To:** (press and hold the **Shift** key to type a capital T, and the colon).

2 Press **Tab** two times, and then type **Client Services Department**.

3 Press **Enter** to move to the next line.

4 Type the remaining headings, pressing **Tab** after the colon and **Enter** at the end of each line.

5 Press **Enter** two times to insert two blank lines, and then type the body of the memo.

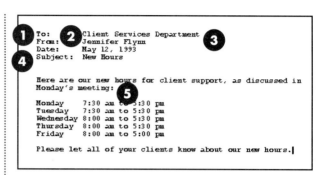

```
To:      Client Services Department
From:    Jennifer Flynn
Date:    May 12, 1993
Subject: New Hours


Here are our new hours for client support, as discussed in
Monday's meeting:

Monday     7:30 am to 5:30 pm
Tuesday    7:30 am to 5:30 pm
Wednesday  8:00 am to 5:30 pm
Thursday   8:00 am to 5:30 pm
Friday     8:00 am to 5:00 pm

Please let all of your clients know about our new hours.
```

TIP

When you begin typing, you may notice your mouse pointer disappears. Don't worry—it's still there.

Just move the mouse, and the pointer will reappear.

ZOOMING IN AND OUT

Why Zoom In or Out?

When working in a document, you may sometimes want to zoom in to see some detail closely, or zoom out to get an overview of how the document will look. WordPerfect offers several options for viewing your document:

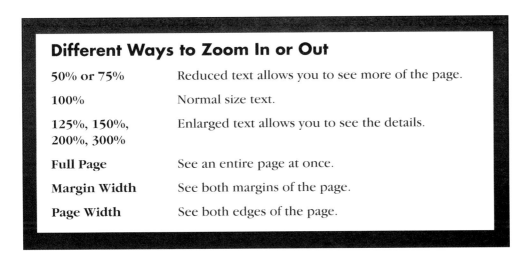

Different Ways to Zoom In or Out

50% or 75%	Reduced text allows you to see more of the page.
100%	Normal size text.
125%, 150%, 200%, 300%	Enlarged text allows you to see the details.
Full Page	See an entire page at once.
Margin Width	See both margins of the page.
Page Width	See both edges of the page.

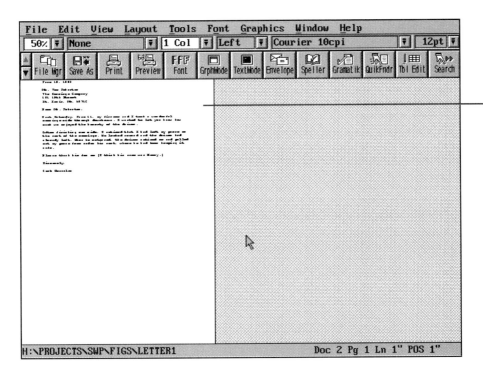

Reduce the size of text to see more of the page.

ZOOMING IN AND OUT

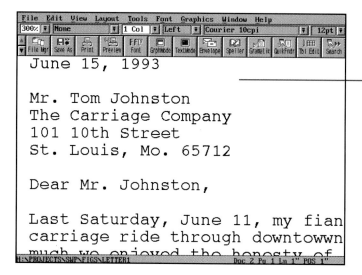

Enlarge the size of text to see details.

TIP

You must be in either Graphics or Full Page Mode to use this task. See the "Changing Viewing Modes" task in Part I (for Graphics Mode) or the "Previewing a Document Before You Print It" task in Part III (for Page Mode).

Zooming In and Out

1 Click on **View**, or press **Alt+V**.

2 Click on **Z**oom, or press **Z**.

3 Choose a viewing mode.

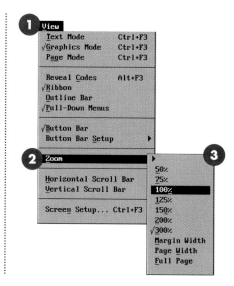

CORRECTING TEXT

How Do You Correct Text?

One of the most marvelous things about using a word processor to type a letter is that when you make a mistake, you don't have to type the entire letter all over (like you would if you had used a typewriter). You can erase text with the Backspace and Delete keys. You can also correct text by typing over it. Normally, the text you type is inserted into a paragraph beginning at the insertion point (the cursor).

If you want to type over text, move the cursor just to the left of the text to type over, and then press the **Insert** key and you'll be in *Overtype Mode*. What you type will replace existing characters on the screen. Press **Insert** again, and you are returned to *Insert Mode*, which is the default for typing text.

Important Keys for Editing Text

BACKSPACE	Use this key to back up and erase text.
DELETE	Use this key to delete a character at the current cursor position.
INSERT	Use this key to toggle between Insert and Overtype Mode.

When you are in Overtype Mode, you will see this message displayed on the Status Line.

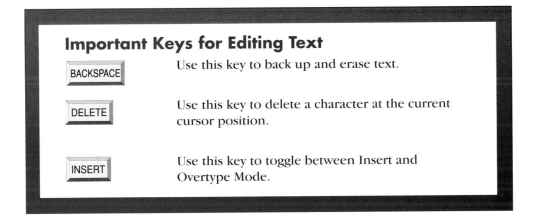

Typeover   Doc 3 Pg 1 Ln 4.17" Pos 5.6"

Status Line

To move the cursor, click anywhere within your document. To move the cursor with the keyboard, use the table on the next page.

Creating and Editing Documents

CORRECTING TEXT

Moving the Cursor

To move	Press
Left or right one character	[←] or [→]
Up or down one line	[↑] or [↓]
Beginning of a line	[HOME] + [←]
End of a line	[HOME] + [→] or [END]
One word left or right	[CTRL] + [←] or [→]
One paragraph up or down	[CTRL] + [↑] or [↓]
Up or down one page	[PG UP] or [PG DN]
Top or bottom of a page	[CTRL] + [HOME] + [↑] or [↓]
Specific page	[CTRL] + [HOME], then enter page number
Top or bottom of screen	[HOME] + [↑] or [↓]
Beginning of document	[HOME] + [HOME] + [↑]
End of document	[HOME] + [HOME] + [↓]

There are some additional ways to move around a document, depending on your display. See the "Working with Multiple Documents" task in Part III for more information.

TIP

You can delete a word by placing the cursor in the word and pressing **Ctrl+Backspace**.

If you want to delete large blocks of text, see the "Deleting Selected Text" or the "Selecting Blocks of Text" tasks later in this part.

LEARNING THE LINGO

Overtype Mode: The opposite of *Insert Mode*. In Overtype Mode, what you type replaces existing characters.

Insert Mode: The default typing mode. When you position your cursor and start to type using Insert Mode, what you type is inserted at that point and existing text is pushed to the right.

Correcting Text

1 Move the cursor to the place where you want to delete text (see the Tip for information on how to move the cursor).

2 Press **Delete** to delete a character at the cursor.

OR

Press **Backspace** to erase characters to the left of the cursor.

OR

Press **Insert** to change to Overtype Mode so that what you type will replace existing characters.

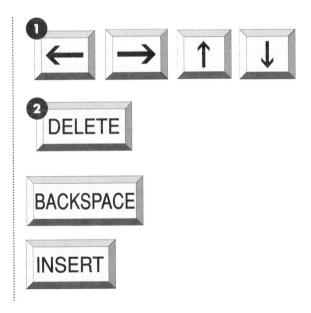

QUICK REFRESHER

To use a shortcut key combination, press and hold the first key and then press the second key. For example, to move to the end of a line, press and hold HOME and then press →.

Creating and Editing Documents

CORRECTING TEXT

Exercise

First, type the letter shown here. Then follow these steps to correct the misspelling and to add some additional text.

1 After finishing the letter, press **Ctrl+Up Arrow** four times to move to the P in Please.

2 Press **End** and then the **Right Arrow** three times to move to the word **sent**.

3 Press the **Backspace** key to erase the letter t and change it to d as in **send**.

4 Use the arrow keys to move in front of the period in the first sentence.

5 Insert the words, **effective with this month's issue**.

```
Attn: Subscription Office

Please cancel my subscription to your magazine. You may sent my
refund to this address:

Jennifer Flynn
10 West 200th
Cloutall, Ohio 43212
```

TIP

You can also click within the document to move the insertion point, instead of pressing the cursor movement keys listed in the exercise.

SELECTING A SENTENCE, PARAGRAPH, OR PAGE

As you edit your documents, you'll probably begin by modifying sections of text. For example, you may want to move a sentence from the beginning of a paragraph to the end. You can move, copy, and delete text by selecting that text and then performing certain commands. In this task, you'll learn how to select an entire sentence, paragraph, or page in a few simple steps.

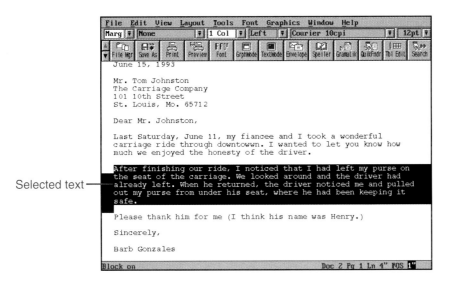

Selected text →

Selected text appears in reverse video. You can select other amounts of text in text blocks. See the "Selecting Blocks of Text" task later in this part.

LEARNING THE LINGO

Formatting: The process of changing the look of a character (by making it bold, underlined, and slightly bigger, for example) or a paragraph (by centering the paragraph between the margins or by adding an automatic indentation for the first line, for example).

TIP

After selecting a sentence, paragraph, or page, you can copy, move, or delete it by following the instructions in later tasks in this part. Using tasks found in later parts, you can also *format*, spell check, print, or save any amount of selected text.

SELECTING A SENTENCE, PARAGRAPH, OR PAGE

Selecting a Sentence, Paragraph, or Page

1 Move the cursor just to the left of the block of text to select.

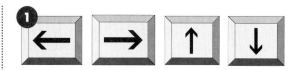

2 Open the **Edit** menu by clicking on it, or pressing **Alt+E**.

3 Click on the **Select** command, or press **S**.

4 Click on either **Sentence**, **Paragraph**, or **Page**, or press **S**, **P**, or **A**.

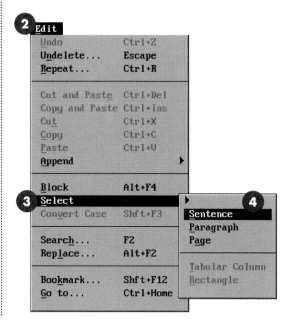

SELECTING BLOCKS OF TEXT

Why Select Text in Blocks?

Sometimes you may want to copy, move, or delete an amount of text that is not a sentence, paragraph, or page. Text *blocks* can be of any size, so they allow you complete freedom manipulating text in your document.

LEARNING THE LINGO

Block: Any amount of selected text.

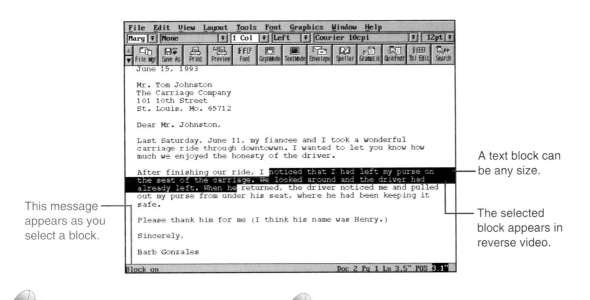

This message appears as you select a block.

A text block can be any size.

The selected block appears in reverse video.

TIP

If you selected a block of text by accident, simply click anywhere in the document, or press **Esc**.

You can also press **F12** to initiate text blocking.

TIP

After selecting a block of text, you can copy, move, or delete it by following the instructions in later tasks in this part. Using tasks found in later parts, you can also *format*, spell check, print, or save any amount of selected text.

Creating and Editing Documents

SELECTING BLOCKS OF TEXT

Selecting Blocks of Text

1 Move the cursor to the first character that you would like to select.

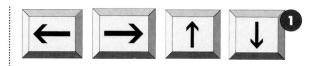

2 Click and hold the left mouse button, or press **Alt+F4**.

3 Drag the mouse pointer, or use the cursor movement keys to move to the last character you want to select.

QUICK REFRESHER

You can use the cursor movement keys to quickly block text with the keyboard. First, press **Alt+F4** or **F12** to initiate text blocking. Then select any of the cursor movement keys:

To block this text	Press this
One character at a time	← or →
One line at a time	↑ or ↓
One word at a time	CTRL + ← or →
One paragraph at a time	CTRL + ↑ or ↓
One page at a time	PG UP or PG DN

See the "Correcting Text" task in this part for additional cursor movement keys to try.

DELETING SELECTED TEXT

When Should You Delete Selected Text?

If you need to make drastic changes to a letter, memo, or report, using the Backspace or even the Delete key can be a time-consuming process. Here you'll learn how to get rid of those unwanted words quickly and painlessly.

To delete a section of text, you must select it first. To learn how to select text, see the "Selecting a Sentence, Paragraph, or Page" and "Selecting Blocks of Text" tasks earlier in this part.

Deleting Selected Text

1 Select any amount of text.

Bring your swimsuits – it looks like it's going to be real hot, and the park has a water slide and a pool. Hope to see you there!

1

2 Press **Delete**.

DELETE **2**

QUICK REFRESHER

Here are some common cursor movement keys:

Left or right one character

← or →

Up or down one line

↑ or ↓

Beginning of a line

HOME + ←

End of a line

HOME + → or END

One word left or right

CTRL + ← or →

One paragraph up or down

CTRL + ↑ or ↓

You can also click within the document to move the insertion point, instead of pressing the cursor movement keys listed in the exercise.

45

Creating and Editing Documents

DELETING SELECTED TEXT

TIP

You can delete just a word by placing the cursor in the word and pressing **Ctrl+Backspace**.

Exercise

Type the memo shown here, and practice selecting and deleting text.

1 Select the last sentence in the first paragraph by using the **Edit Sentence** command.

2 Press **Delete**.

3 Select the words **Bring your swimsuits** by dragging over them or pressing **F12** and using the arrow keys to select the block.

4 Press **Delete.**

On Friday, meet in the parking lot at 8:30. We will then form a caravan to the Spring Mills Amusement Park.

Bring your swimsuits - it looks like it's going to be real hot, and the park has a water slide and a pool. Hope to see you there!

UNDELETING TEXT

When Can You Undelete Text?

WordPerfect remembers the last three segments of text you deleted, and you can "undelete" them anytime until you exit WordPerfect. When you undelete text, it is restored to the current cursor location (which may not be the same location that it was deleted from). So keep the cursor location in mind as you use the Undelete command. The Undelete command displays a dialog box that lets you specify which segment of text to insert at the cursor.

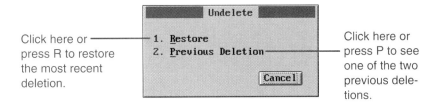

Click here or press R to restore the most recent deletion.

Click here or press P to see one of the two previous deletions.

TIP

WordPerfect has a command called **U**ndo, which is used to "undo" the last change to a document. This includes not only text deletions, but text *formatting* as well. To learn more, see the "Selecting a Menu Command" task in Part I. If you use the **U**ndo command to restore deleted text, the text will be restored to its original location, unlike the Undelete command which restores text to the current cursor location.

(You can only use **U**ndo to restore deleted text if it was the *last* command you performed.)

LEARNING THE LINGO

Formatting: The process of changing the look of a character (by making it bold, underlined, and slightly bigger, for example) or a paragraph (by centering the paragraph between the margins or by adding an automatic indentation for the first line, for example).

Undeleting Text

1 Move the cursor to the text's original location.

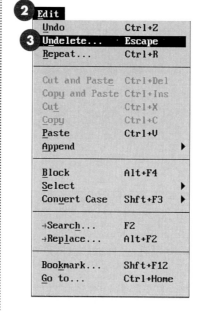

2 Click on Edit, or press **Alt+E**.

3 Click on Undelete, or press **N**.

Edit	
Undo	Ctrl+Z
Undelete...	Escape
Repeat...	Ctrl+R
Cut and Paste	Ctrl+Del
Copy and Paste	Ctrl+Ins
Cut	Ctrl+X
Copy	Ctrl+C
Paste	Ctrl+V
Append	▶
Block	Alt+F4
Select	▶
Convert Case	Shft+F3 ▶
→Search...	F2
→Replace...	Alt+F2
Bookmark...	Shft+F12
Go to...	Ctrl+Home

4 Choose an undelete option. Text is restored at the current cursor location.

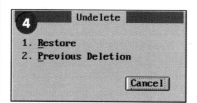

Undelete

1. **R**estore
2. **P**revious Deletion

Cancel

TIP

Instead of using the U**n**delete command to insert the deleted text at the cursor location, you can quickly undelete text by pressing **Esc**.

INSERTING A DATE

Why Insert a Date?

If you often revise your documents, including a date will allow you to track revisions. When you insert a date into your document, WordPerfect updates the date automatically whenever you open that document for changes or print it. That's because this procedure inserts a *date code* that the computer can update. You also can insert a date that does not change, if you want. In this case, you would be inserting *date text* that would be equivalent to manually typing the date.

Regardless of whether you insert a date code or date text, they will both display within your document as a normal date. You can change the format of the date if you like. (See the Tip for this task.)

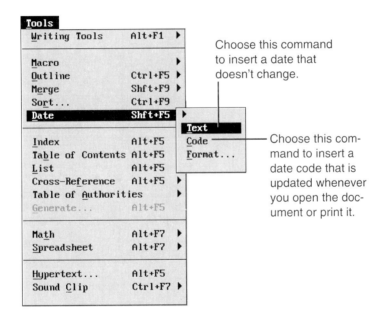

Choose this command to insert a date that doesn't change.

Choose this command to insert a date code that is updated whenever you open the document or print it.

LEARNING THE LINGO

Date code: An invisible code that represents the current date. This code is changed whenever you open a document for changes, or print it.

Date text: Text that WordPerfect can insert for you; use this instead of typing the date. Date text is not updated as changes are made to the document.

Creating and Editing Documents

INSERTING A DATE

Inserting a Date

1 Place the cursor where you would like to insert a date.

2 Click on the **Tools** menu, or press **Alt+T**.

3 Click on **Date**, or press **D**.

4 Click on either **Text** or **Code**, or press **T** or **C**.

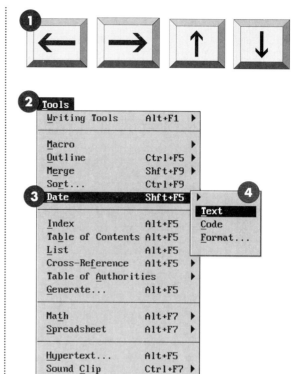

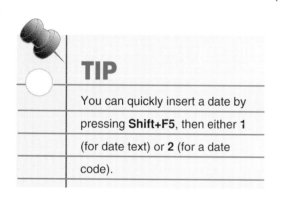

TIP

You can quickly insert a date by pressing **Shift+F5**, then either **1** (for date text) or **2** (for a date code).

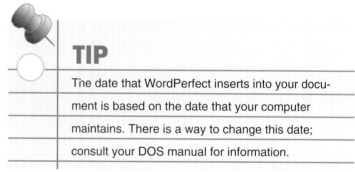

TIP

The date that WordPerfect inserts into your document is based on the date that your computer maintains. There is a way to change this date; consult your DOS manual for information.

50

TIP

To change the format of dates before you insert them, follow steps 1–3, and at step 4, click on
Format, or press **F**. Choose an option, and click **OK** or press **Enter**. The format you choose will
remain effective until you exit WordPerfect.

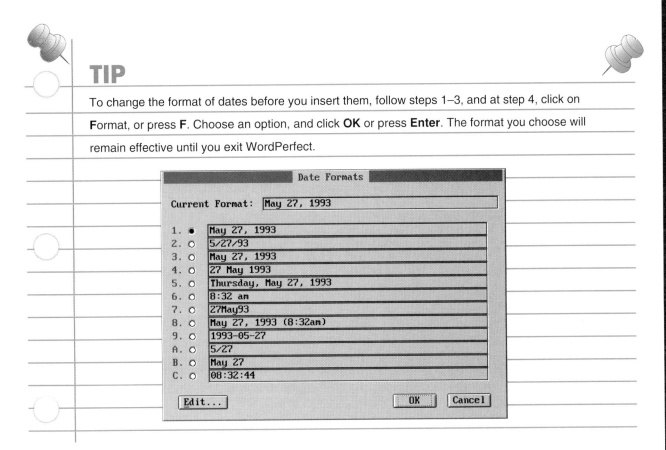

COPYING AND MOVING TEXT

Why Copy or Move Text?

Most of the time spent in creating a document is spent in editing: copying, moving, and deleting text to fine-tune your document. The ability to copy and move text is a big timesaver, and one of the things that makes using a computer a real joy.

For example, suppose you wanted to move several paragraphs from the beginning of a document to the end. If WordPerfect did not provide the ability to move text, you would have to delete the paragraphs at the beginning of the document and retype them at the end.

LEARNING THE LINGO

Copying text: When you copy text, the selected text stays in its original location, and a copy of the selected text is placed where you indicate.

Moving text: When you move text, the selected text is deleted from its original location and moved to where you indicate.

TIP

You can perform similar steps to copy and move text between documents. See the "Copying and Moving Text Between Documents" task in Part III.

Copying and Moving Text

1 Select the text you want to copy or move.

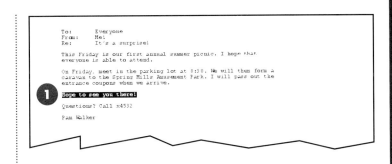

2 Click on Edit, or press **Alt+E**.

3 To copy text, click on Copy and Paste, or press **Y**. To move text, click on Cut and Paste, or press **E**.

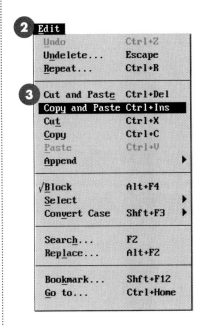

4 Move the cursor to where you would like to place the selected text.

5 Press **Enter**.

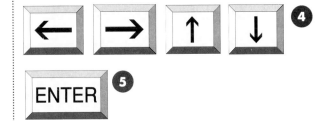

53

COPYING AND MOVING TEXT

Exercise

Type the text shown here, and then follow these steps.

1 Select the last paragraph. Click on **Edit**, or press **Alt+E**.

2 Click on **Cut and Paste**, or press **E**.

3 Move to the top of the page. Press **Enter**.

4 Select **July 12 Picnic in the Park**.

5 Click on **Edit**, or press **Alt+E**.

6 Click on **Copy and Paste**, or press **Y**.

7 Move to the bottom of the page. Press **Enter**.

> The following is a list of upcoming events:
>
> July 12   Picnic in the Park
> July 18   Concert Under the Stars
> July 23   Backyard Bar-B-Que
>
> The Ellentown Arts League thanks you for your donation, and we invite you to attend the many exciting events we have planned!

STARTING A NEW PAGE

Why Start a New Page?

Normally, you don't have to tell WordPerfect to start a new page; when the text you enter fills a page, WordPerfect automatically starts a new page for you. When WordPerfect starts a new page, something called a *soft page break* is inserted. If you want some text to start at the top of a new page (in order to separate big sections in a report, for example), you must insert a *hard page break*.

Unlike a soft page break that adjusts as text is entered or deleted, a hard page break stays with the text where it was entered, and forces that text to start on a new page regardless of any editing changes.

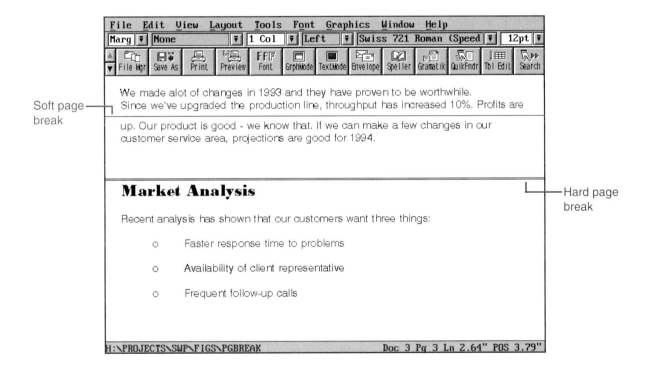

Soft page break

Hard page break

LEARNING THE LINGO

Hard page break: An invisible code that, when inserted into a document at a particular point, tells WordPerfect to begin a new page (even if the preceding page is not full).

Soft page break: The opposite of a hard page break. This is an invisible code that WordPerfect inserts automatically when text fills a page and a new page must be started.

Creating and Editing Documents

STARTING A NEW PAGE

Inserting a Hard Page Break

1 Move to the place where you would like to insert a hard page break.

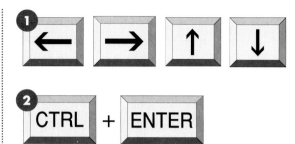

2 Press **Ctrl+Enter**.

TIP

If you want to delete a hard page break, move the insertion point to the first letter on the page and press **Backspace**. To see where the invisible hard page break code is, you can turn on Reveal Codes.

See the "Revealing Formatting Codes" task in Part IV.

SEARCHING FOR TEXT

Why Search for Text?

Sometimes you may want to locate a specific section of a document. For example, if you want to make changes to a specific part of a long report, you can search for the title of that section. You can also search for hidden formatting codes, such as the beginning or end of a section of bold text. For more information on these hidden codes, see the "Revealing Formatting Codes" task in Part IV.

When WordPerfect searches your document, it begins at the current cursor location and searches either forward (toward the end of your document) or backward (toward the beginning of your document). Once a match is found, the search is ended, but you can repeat the search again in order to find the next occurrence of a word.

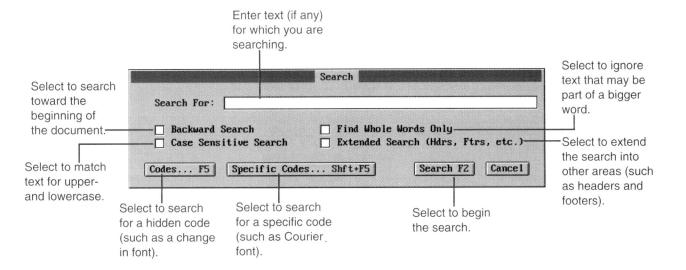

Enter text (if any) for which you are searching.

Select to ignore text that may be part of a bigger word.

Select to search toward the beginning of the document.

Select to match text for upper- and lowercase.

Select to search for a hidden code (such as a change in font).

Select to search for a specific code (such as Courier font).

Select to begin the search.

Select to extend the search into other areas (such as headers and footers).

SEARCHING FOR TEXT

Searching for Text

1 Move the insertion point to the place where you would like to start the search. To move to the beginning of the document, press **Home**, **Home**, and then the **up arrow**.

2 Click on the Edit menu, or press **Alt+E**.

3 Click on Search, or press **H**.

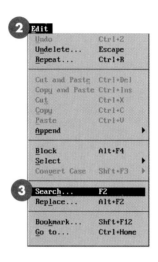

4 Select the search options in the Search dialog box.

5 Click on **Search**, or press **F2** to begin the search.

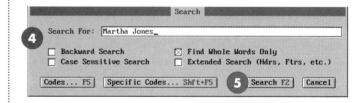

6 If you want, repeat the exact same search by pressing **F2** twice.

TIP

You can quickly initiate a search by pressing **F2**. Also, when a search is successful, the insertion point will be moved to the search point. To return to your original cursor position, press **Ctrl+Home** two times.

REPLACING TEXT

Why Replace Text?

Instead of simply searching for text, you can search and replace text in one step. You might want to use this option to change the name of something or someone (such as a contact name or phone number used frequently in a welcome letter).

When the search is successful, the dialog box shown here will appear; use it to tell WordPerfect what to do. WordPerfect will continue searching and replacing until the entire document is searched, or you cancel the search.

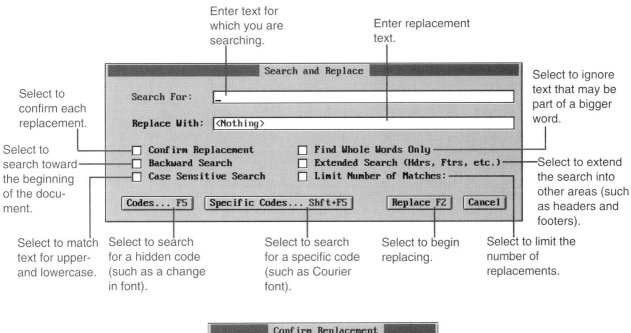

Enter text for which you are searching.

Enter replacement text.

Select to ignore text that may be part of a bigger word.

Select to confirm each replacement.

Select to search toward the beginning of the document.

Select to match text for upper- and lowercase.

Select to search for a hidden code (such as a change in font).

Select to search for a specific code (such as Courier font).

Select to begin replacing.

Select to extend the search into other areas (such as headers and footers).

Select to limit the number of replacements.

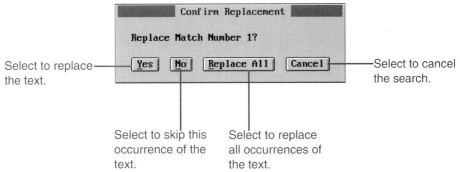

Select to replace the text.

Select to cancel the search.

Select to skip this occurrence of the text.

Select to replace all occurrences of the text.

Creating and Editing Documents

REPLACING TEXT

Searching For Text

1 Move the insertion point to the place where you want to start the replacement. To move to the beginning of the document, press **Home**, **Home**, and then the **up arrow**.

2 Click on the **Edit** menu, or press **Alt+E**.

3 Click on Replace, or press **L**.

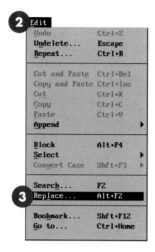

4 Select the search and replace options.

5 Click on **Replace**, or press **F2** to begin the search.

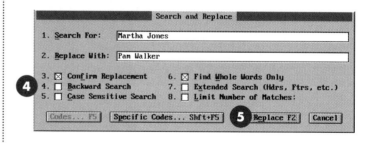

6 Select a replacement option from the dialog box that appears.

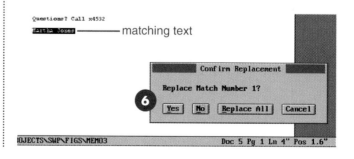

PART 3

Opening, Saving, and Printing Documents

In this part, you will learn the basics of working with documents: opening existing documents, saving your work, and printing documents. You will also learn how to close (put away) a document after you are finished working with it.

- Opening an Existing Document
- Starting a New Document
- Saving a Document and Continuing to Work
- Saving a Document and Closing It
- Saving Documents Automatically
- Using File Manager to Manage Your Files
- Locating a Document with File Manager
- Using Quick List to Add Personal Directories
- Working with Multiple Documents
- Copying or Moving Text Between Documents
- Previewing a Document Before You Print It
- Printing a Document

OPENING AN EXISTING DOCUMENT

When Can You Open an Existing Document?

Anytime you want to make changes to a document that you've saved and closed (put away), you must reopen it. In order to tell WordPerfect to open a particular document, you must pick its name from a list. When you save a document, give it a file name that describes the document's contents. Documents are stored in *directories*; you can create your own directory just for your documents, or you can place your documents in the WordPerfect directory. Using the **File Open** command causes WordPerfect to ask you for more information.

Select to open document into its own window.

Enter a file name, or open the drop-down list box to display a list of file names to open.

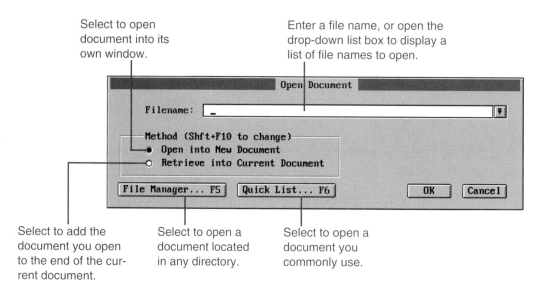

Select to add the document you open to the end of the current document.

Select to open a document located in any directory.

Select to open a document you commonly use.

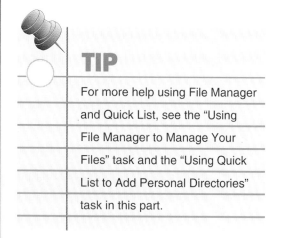

TIP

For more help using File Manager and Quick List, see the "Using File Manager to Manage Your Files" task and the "Using Quick List to Add Personal Directories" task in this part.

LEARNING THE LINGO

File name: A name for a file that consists of a first name of up to eight characters and an optional *extension*. These are valid file names: BUDGET93.DOC, JAN3.MEM, APRSALES.RPT, and MOM.LTR.

Extension: The part of a file name after the period that consists of up to three letters. The extension describes the type of file or the program in which it was created. For example, an extension of .LTR may mean letter.

Directory: Because large hard disks can store thousands of files, you need directories to store related files. Think of your disk as a filing cabinet and think of each directory as a drawer in the filing cabinet. By keeping files in separate directories, you can easily locate and work with related files.

Opening an Existing Document

1 Click on the File menu, or press **Alt+F**.

2 Click on Open, or press **O**.

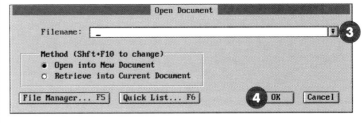

3 Click on the down arrow to the right of the Filename drop-down list box, then click on a file name to select it. If you use the keyboard, press the down arrow key, and use it to highlight a file to open.

4 Click on **OK**, or press **Enter** to open the file.

TIP

You can quickly open a file by pressing **Shift+F10**.

If WordPerfect can't locate the document you are trying to open, an error message will be issued.

Check your spelling or use the File Manager to locate your file. See the "Using File Manager to

Manage Your Files" task later in this part.

Opening, Saving, and Printing Documents

STARTING A NEW DOCUMENT

When Should You Start a New Document?

When you start WordPerfect, a blank (new) document is provided for you. But what should you do when you finish one document and you want to start another? Answer: you open a new document.

Opening a new document displays a new, blank document text area on your screen. Before you open a new document, you may want to save your previous document and close it (put it away). See the "Saving a Document and Closing It" task later in this part.

Starting a New Document

1 Click on the **F**ile menu, or press **Alt+F**.

2 Click on **N**ew, or press **N**.

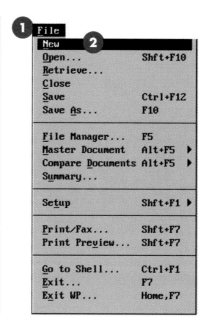

SAVING A DOCUMENT AND CONTINUING TO WORK

When Is Saving Necessary?

You'll always need to save your document prior to exiting WordPerfect (because otherwise, you'll lose your changes). But, you should also use the File Save command to save your document periodically during a long work session. In addition, you should save your documents right before you make major changes to a document, perform a search and replace, or print a document. (You can configure WordPerfect to automatically save your documents for you at periodic intervals. See the "Saving Documents Automatically" task later in this part.)

When you save a file, you give it a file name of up to eight characters. You should also include an extension of up to three characters. Separate the file name from the extension with a period, as in COHOURS.DOC. If you continue working on a file after you've saved it, remember to save the file again before you exit WordPerfect.

Enter file name for document.

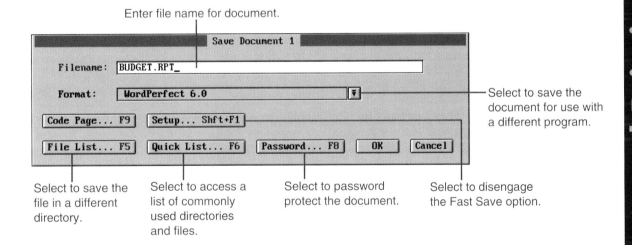

Select to save the document for use with a different program.

Select to save the file in a different directory.

Select to access a list of commonly used directories and files.

Select to password protect the document.

Select to disengage the Fast Save option.

TIP

For more help using File List (File Manager) and Quick List, see the "Using File Manager to Manage Your Files" task and the "Using Quick List to Add Personal Directories" task in this part.

65

LEARNING THE LINGO

File name: A name for a file that consists of a first name of up to eight characters and an optional *extension*. These are valid file names: BUDGET93.DOC, JAN3.MEM, APRSALES.RPT, and MOM.LTR.

Extension: The part of a file name after the period that consists of up to three letters. The extension describes the type of file or the program in which it was created. For example, an extension of .LTR might mean letter.

Directory: Because large hard disks can store thousands of files, you need directories to store related files. Think of your disk as a filing cabinet and think of each directory as a drawer in the filing cabinet. By keeping files in separate directories, you can easily locate and work with related files.

Fast save: An option that reduces the amount of time necessary to save a file during a work session.

Saving a Document and Continuing to Work

1 Click on the **File** menu, or press **Alt+F**.

2 Click on Save **As**, or press **A**.

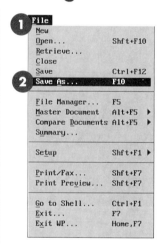

3 If this is the first time you've saved this document, or if you want to save this document under a new name, enter a name for the file.

4 Select any additional options you want.

5 Click on **OK**, or press **Enter** to save the file.

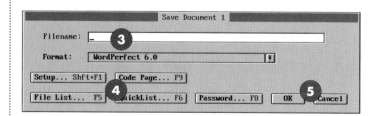

6 If this file has been saved before, you'll be asked if you want to replace it. Click on **Yes**, or press **Y**.

Replace H:\PROJECTS\SWP\FIGS\MEMO4?

6 Yes   No

TIP

To enter a password, press **F8** while in the Save Document dialog box. Enter any password, up to 23 characters. When you open the document later on, you'll be prompted for the password. If you want to remove the password, choose **Password** (from within the Save Document dialog box) to access the Password dialog, and then press **F6**.

TIP

To save a document quickly, you can press **F10** or click on the **Save As** button on the Button Bar.

You can also quickly save already saved documents by using the **F**ile **S**ave command. When you use this command, you will not be asked if you want to replace the file; the file will simply be overlaid.

Exercise

Follow these steps to create a new document and save it.

1 Click on the File menu, or press **Alt+F**.

2 Click on **New**, or press **N**.

3 Type in any amount of text.

4 Click on **Save As** on the Button Bar.

5 Enter the file name **TEST.DOC**.

6 Click **OK**, or press **Enter**.

Opening, Saving, and Printing Documents

SAVING A DOCUMENT AND CLOSING IT

Why Close Documents?

After you are through with a document, you should close it (put it away). Remembering to close documents when you are done with them helps to eliminate clutter and makes it easier to work. After you close a document, you can also exit WordPerfect at the same time, or you can open another document and start working on it. Use the **File Exit** command to tell WordPerfect to close a document, and then tell WordPerfect whether or not you want to exit.

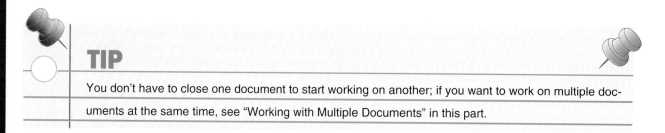

TIP

You don't have to close one document to start working on another; if you want to work on multiple documents at the same time, see "Working with Multiple Documents" in this part.

Saving a Document and Closing It

1 Click on the File menu, or press **Alt+F**.

2 Click on **Exit**, or press **E**.

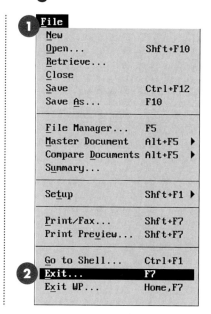

3 Decide whether to save the document or not.

4 Decide whether to exit WordPerfect or not.

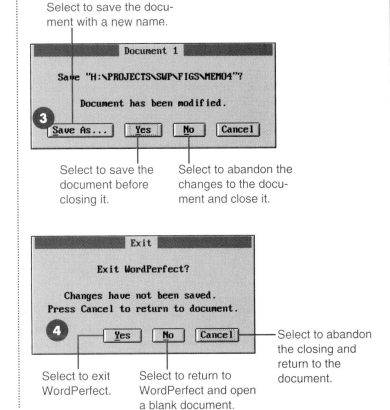

Select to save the document with a new name.

Document 1

Save "H:\PROJECTS\SWP\FIGS\MEMO4"?

Document has been modified.

3 [Save As...] [Yes] [No] [Cancel]

Select to save the document before closing it.

Select to abandon the changes to the document and close it.

Exit

Exit WordPerfect?

Changes have not been saved.
Press Cancel to return to document.

4 [Yes] [No] [Cancel]

Select to abandon the closing and return to the document.

Select to exit WordPerfect.

Select to return to WordPerfect and open a blank document.

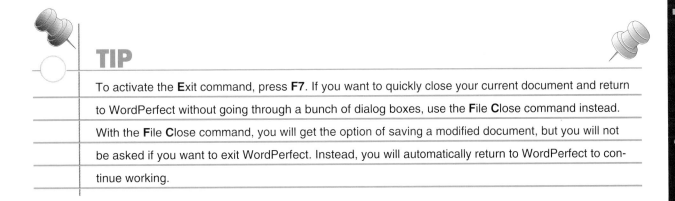

TIP

To activate the **E**xit command, press **F7**. If you want to quickly close your current document and return to WordPerfect without going through a bunch of dialog boxes, use the **F**ile **C**lose command instead. With the **F**ile **C**lose command, you will get the option of saving a modified document, but you will not be asked if you want to exit WordPerfect. Instead, you will automatically return to WordPerfect to continue working.

Opening, Saving, and Printing Documents

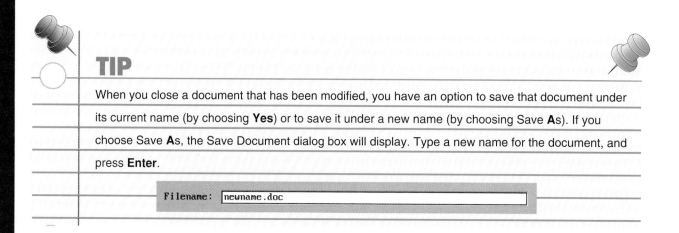

TIP

When you close a document that has been modified, you have an option to save that document under its current name (by choosing **Yes**) or to save it under a new name (by choosing Save **A**s). If you choose Save **A**s, the Save Document dialog box will display. Type a new name for the document, and press **Enter**.

Filename: newname.doc

Exercise

Use the TEST.DOC file you created in the exercise in the "Saving a Document and Continuing to Work" task to complete this exercise. If necessary, complete that exercise now. If you've already closed the file, use the **File Open** command to reopen it.

1 Type some additional text into the TEST.DOC file.

2 Click on the **File** menu, or press **Alt+F**.

3 Click on **Exit**, or press **E**.

4 Click on **Yes** to save the changes.

5 Click on **No** to remain in WordPerfect.

SAVING DOCUMENTS AUTOMATICALLY

Why Save Automatically?

By saving your documents often, you can save yourself a lot of time and trouble if something happens to your computer (such as a power failure). Knowing that you should save your documents frequently is one thing, remembering to do it is another. If you don't want to bother with remembering to save files often, you can tell WordPerfect to periodically save your work for you with the Backup dialog box.

When WordPerfect saves your document for you, it can also save the original unchanged version. Usually, when WordPerfect saves a document that has been modified, it overlays the original version of that file. If you select the **Back Up Original Document** option, WordPerfect will save the previously saved version of the document with an extension **(.BK!)**; that way, you can return to the unchanged version of a document you've recently modified.

Select to activate automatic backups.

Select if you want WordPerfect to save the unchanged version of your document when you save the changes or exit.

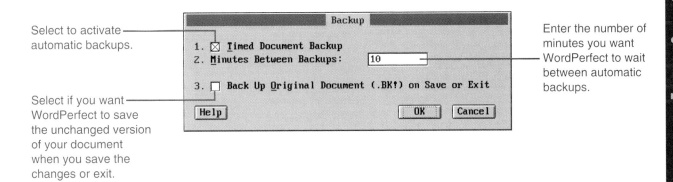

Enter the number of minutes you want WordPerfect to wait between automatic backups.

LEARNING THE LINGO

Document backup: Saving your document in periodic intervals as you continue to work.

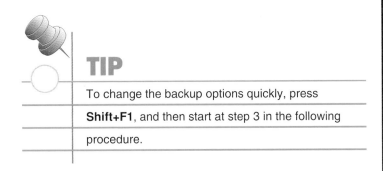

TIP

To change the backup options quickly, press **Shift+F1**, and then start at step 3 in the following procedure.

Saving Documents Automatically

1 Click on the **File** menu, or press **Alt+F**.

2 Click on **Setup**, or press **T**.

3 Click on **Environment**, or press **E**.

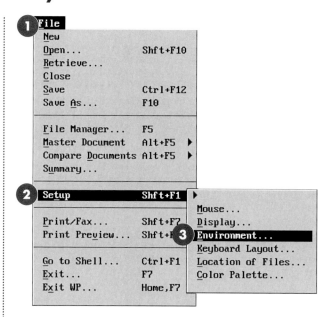

4 Click on **Backup Options**, or press **B**.

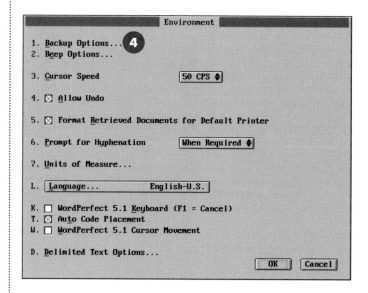

5 Select backup options.

6 Click on **OK**, or press **Enter**.

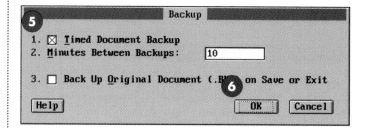

USING FILE MANAGER TO MANAGE YOUR FILES

Why Use File Manager?

File Manager provides many ways to manage your documents. For example, you can use File Manager to search for a document, to view a document before opening it, or to print multiple documents at one time, among other things.

After opening File Manager, you select a directory whose files you want to work with in the Specify File Manager List dialog box. In the file list that's displayed in the File Manager dialog box, mark the documents you want to work with. Then select an option, such as **L**ook (to view a document) or **P**rint. In this task, you'll learn how to open File Manager and mark files.

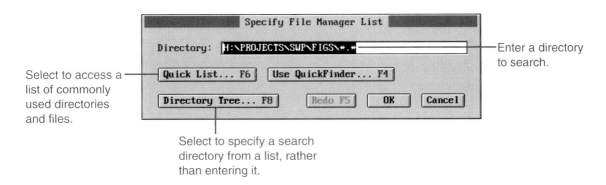

Select to access a list of commonly used directories and files.

Enter a directory to search.

Select to specify a search directory from a list, rather than entering it.

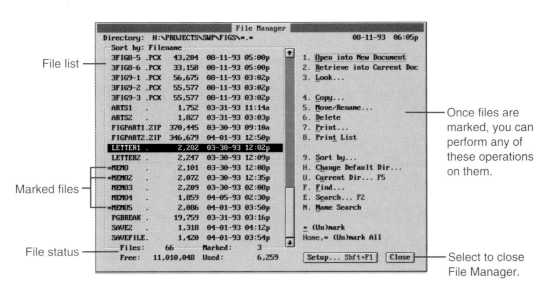

File list

Marked files

File status

Once files are marked, you can perform any of these operations on them.

Select to close File Manager.

73

USING FILE MANAGER TO MANAGE YOUR FILES

Using File Manager

1 Click on the File menu, or press **Alt+F**.

2 Click on File Manager, or press **F**.

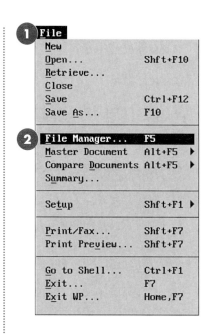

3 Enter the directory to search.

4 Click **OK**, or press **Enter**.

5 Highlight a file by clicking on it or using the arrow keys.

6 Click on **(Un)Mark**, or press * (asterisk).

7 Select an option.

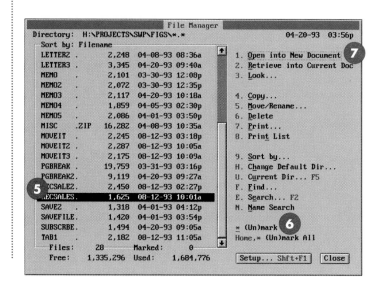

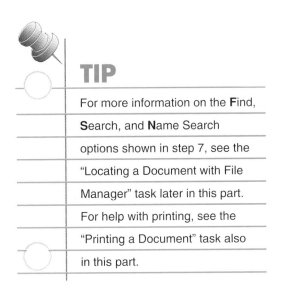

TIP

For more information on the **F**ind, **S**earch, and **N**ame Search options shown in step 7, see the "Locating a Document with File Manager" task later in this part. For help with printing, see the "Printing a Document" task also in this part.

QUICK REFRESHER

File Manager also can be accessed through the Button Bar or through the Open, Save, or Save As dialog boxes (by selecting File Manager or File List).

Opening, Saving, and Printing Documents

LOCATING A DOCUMENT WITH FILE MANAGER

Why Search for a Document?

When you save a file, you give it a unique name of up to eight characters (see the "Saving a Document and Continuing to Work" task earlier in this part). Even if you're clever, it's tough to completely describe each and every document in only eight letters. With File Manager, you can easily locate a document even when you're not sure of its name. You can search for a file two ways: by searching for text within the document, or by searching for all or part of the file name. From within the File Manager window, select the **Find** command, and several options will display, as shown in this table. Keep in mind that when you perform a search using the **Find** command, all the *marked* files in the file listing are searched. (See the "Using File Manager to Manage Your Files" task earlier in this part for information on how to mark files.)

Table: Choosing From Among the Various Find Options

To search	Use this option
For any part of a file name	Name
For text within the Document Summary	Document Summary
Only the first page of each document	First Page
Through all the text within each document	Entire Document
By combining search conditions	Conditions

TIP

To erase your search selections and start over, use the **U**ndo option in the Find dialog box.

LEARNING THE LINGO

Document summary: An optional part of a document where you can store information about the document's type, purpose, author, subject, and so on.

Locating a Document with File Manager

1 Click on the File menu, or press **Alt+F**.

2 Click on File Manager, or press **F**.

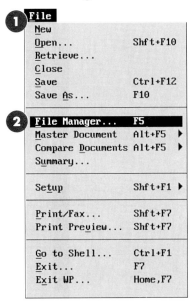

3 Enter the directory for which you want to search.

4 Click on **OK**, or press **Enter**.

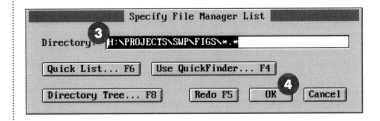

5 Click on Find, or press **F**.

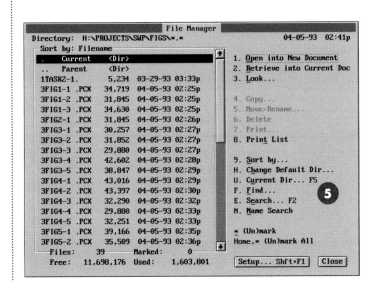

LOCATING A DOCUMENT WITH FILE MANAGER

6 Select a search option.

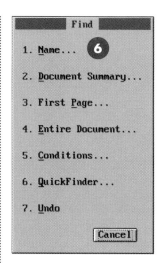

7 Enter either part of the file name, or some text for which you want to search.

8 Click on **OK**, or press **Enter** to begin the search. The file list is modified to display only those documents that match the search criteria.

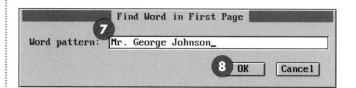

TIP

You can add a summary to any document so you can find it more easily. Use the **F**ile S**u**mmary command, fill in the dialog box, and press **Enter** or click on **OK**.

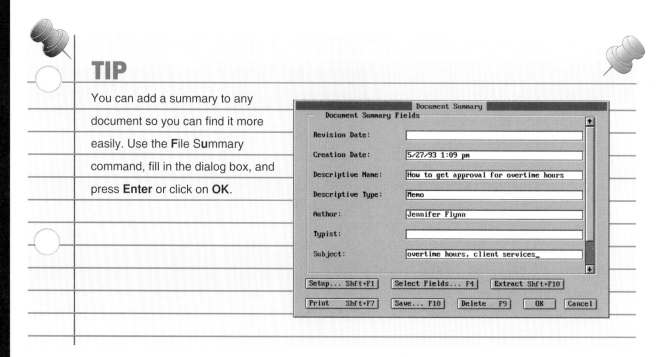

TIP

You can access the File Manager quickly by clicking on the **File Manager** button on the Button Bar.

Exercise

Follow these steps to locate a previously saved document by searching for text which appears on its first page.

1 Click on the **File Manager** button on the Button Bar.

2 Click on **OK**, or press **Enter** to accept the default directory.

3 Click on Find, or press **F**.

4 Click on **First Page**.

5 Enter some text for which you want to search.

6 Click on **OK**, or press **Enter** to begin the search. The file list is modified to display only those documents that match the search criteria.

Opening, Saving, and Printing Documents

USING QUICK LIST TO ADD PERSONAL DIRECTORIES

Why Use Quick List?

Whenever you open or save a file, you are required to tell WordPerfect which *drive* and *directory* to use. If you store your files in many different directories such as SALES, BUDGET, MEMOS, and so on, you can use the Quick List option in File Manager to store the names of these directories so you can refer to them more quickly.

You access Quick List from within File Manager, then enter the names of the directories you use frequently when saving your files. To specify a directory for Quick List, you will need to enter a *directory path*. A directory path consists of a drive letter followed by a colon (as in **C:**), followed by a backslash (\\), followed by a directory name (such as **SALES**). A completed directory path might look like this: **C:\\SALES**.

LEARNING THE LINGO

Drive: A device that writes and reads data on a magnetic disk. Think of a disk drive as being like a cassette recorder/player. Just as the cassette player can record sounds on a magnetic cassette tape and play back those sounds, a disk drive can record data on a magnetic disk and play back that data.

Directory: Because large hard disks can store thousands of files, you need directories to store related files. Think of your disk as a filing cabinet and think of each directory as a drawer in the filing cabinet. By keeping files in separate directories, you can easily locate and work with related files.

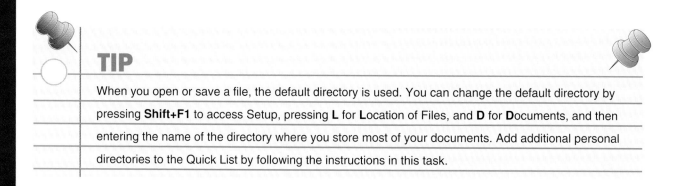

TIP

When you open or save a file, the default directory is used. You can change the default directory by pressing **Shift+F1** to access Setup, pressing **L** for **L**ocation of Files, and **D** for **D**ocuments, and then entering the name of the directory where you store most of your documents. Add additional personal directories to the Quick List by following the instructions in this task.

Adding a Personal Directory to Quick List

1 Click on the File menu, or press **Alt+F**.

2 Click on File Manager, or press **F**.

3 Click on **Quick List**, or press **F6**.

4 Click on Create, or press **C**.

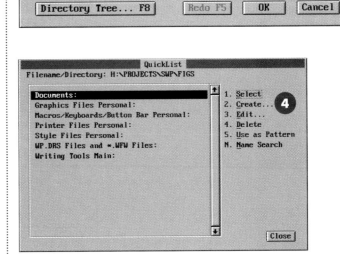

Opening, Saving, and Printing Documents

USING QUICK LIST TO ADD PERSONAL DIRECTORIES

5 Enter a description for the directory.

6 Enter the directory path, or click on **Directory Tree** and select a directory from the list.

7 Click on **OK**, or press **Enter**.

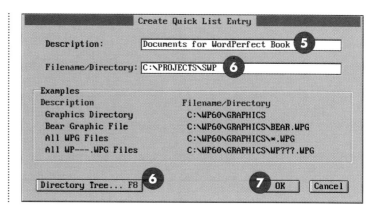

TIP

Once you have added your personal directories to Quick List, you simply click on the **Quick List** button from within the Open Document and Save Document dialog boxes. The Quick List window will appear. Select a personal directory by clicking on it, and then click on **OK** to see a list of files in that directory.

WORKING WITH MULTIPLE DOCUMENTS

When Would You Want to Work with Multiple Documents?

You can open documents one at a time throughout a work session, or you can open several files at once by using the File Manager. (See the "Using File Manager to Manage Your Files" task earlier in this part.) Once several documents are open, you can copy or move text between them, or simply refer to one document as you edit another. You can scroll through each document and make changes as you would at any other time. However, you can only make changes to one document at a time: the *active document*.

Usually, the active document takes up the entire screen, but you can *tile* the document windows or *cascade* them. When you use either of these commands to arrange documents on your screen, the documents are automatically surrounded by a *frame*. You can easily control the exact arrangement of documents on your screen.

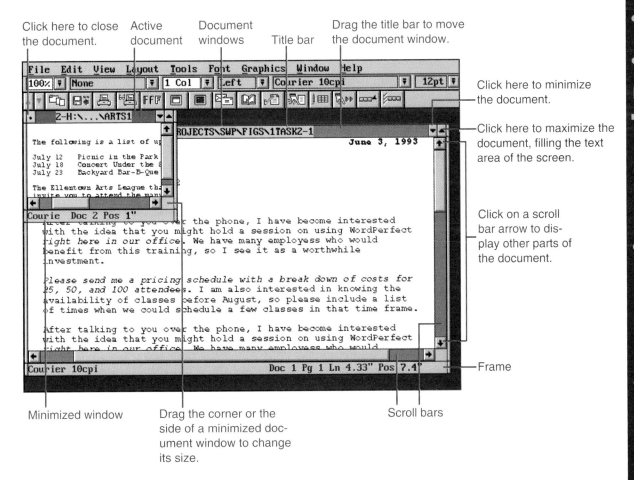

Click here to close the document.

Active document

Document windows

Title bar

Drag the title bar to move the document window.

Click here to minimize the document.

Click here to maximize the document, filling the text area of the screen.

Click on a scroll bar arrow to display other parts of the document.

Frame

Minimized window

Drag the corner or the side of a minimized document window to change its size.

Scroll bars

WORKING WITH MULTIPLE DOCUMENTS

LEARNING THE LINGO

Tile: Dividing the screen equally between all open documents.

Cascade: Arranging documents in an overlapping fashion so that just their title bars show.

Frame: A border that can be placed around a document, which allows you to resize and move the document on-screen.

Scroll bars: Optionally displayed along the bottom and right sides of the document window, scroll bars are used to display other areas of the document.

Working with Multiple Documents

1 With several documents already open, click on **Window**, or press **Alt+W**.

2 Decide how you would like to arrange your open documents.

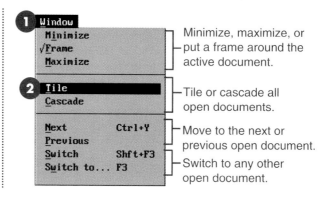

Minimize, maximize, or put a frame around the active document.

Tile or cascade all open documents.

Move to the next or previous open document.

Switch to any other open document.

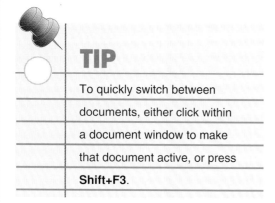

TIP

To quickly switch between documents, either click within a document window to make that document active, or press **Shift+F3**.

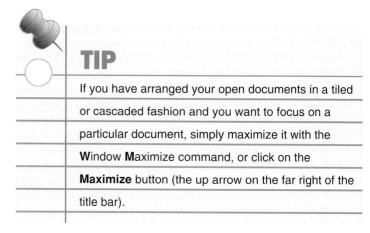

TIP

If you have arranged your open documents in a tiled or cascaded fashion and you want to focus on a particular document, simply maximize it with the **Window Maximize** command, or click on the **Maximize** button (the up arrow on the far right of the title bar).

COPYING OR MOVING TEXT BETWEEN DOCUMENTS

Why Copy or Move Text Between Documents?

When you create many similar documents, the ability to "recycle" text (copy or move text from one document to another) can be a real timesaver. The easiest way to copy or move text between two documents is when the document windows are tiled or cascaded (see the "Working With Multiple Documents" task earlier in this part). However, you can still copy or move text even when the document windows are *maximized*.

For example, if you wanted to write a letter to a client, you could open a previously saved letter and copy the client's name and address into your new document instead of typing it. If you wanted to break a long report into separate documents, you could move text from one document into another.

LEARNING THE LINGO

Copying text: When you copy text, the selected text stays in its original location, and a copy of the selected text is placed where you indicate.

Moving text: When you move text, the selected text is deleted from its original location and moved to where you indicate.

Maximize: To make a document window fill the text area. When you first start WordPerfect, the open document is maximized.

TIP

You can quickly copy, cut, and paste by using these Shortcut Keys:

To do this	Press these keys
Copy	CTRL + C
Cut	CTRL + X
Paste	CTRL + V

In addition, if the areas you want to copy/move from and paste to are visible on the screen, you can use the Copy and Paste or Cut and Paste commands instead. See the "Copying or Moving Text" task in Part II.

Copying or Moving Text Between Documents

1 Select the text you want to copy or move.

2 Click on the **Edit** menu, or press **Alt+E**.

3 To copy text, click on **Copy**, or press **C**. To move text, click on **Cut**, or press **T**.

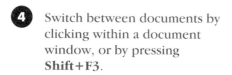

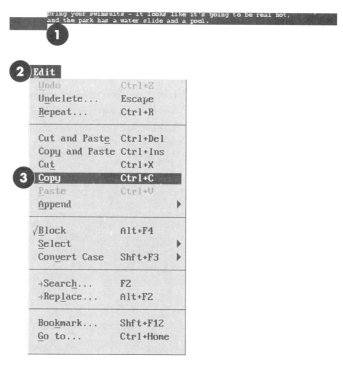

4 Switch between documents by clicking within a document window, or by pressing **Shift+F3**.

5 Move the cursor to where you would like to place the text.

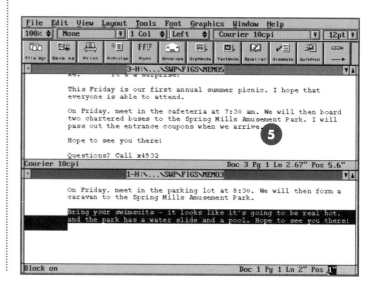

COPYING OR MOVING TEXT BETWEEN DOCUMENTS

6 Click on Edit, or press **Alt+E**.

7 Click on Paste, or press **P**.

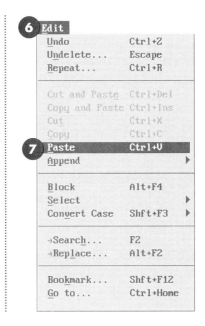

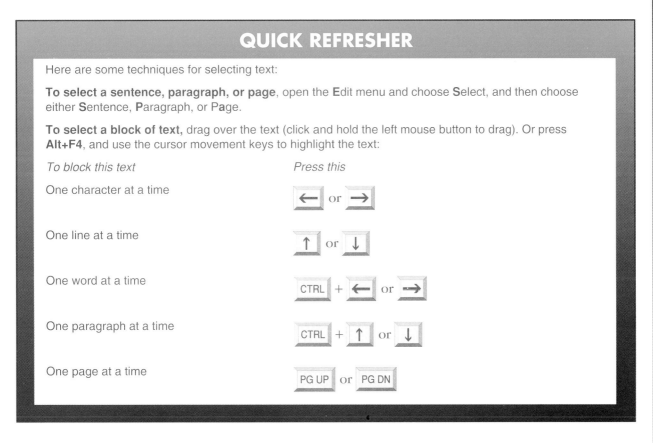

QUICK REFRESHER

Here are some techniques for selecting text:

To select a sentence, paragraph, or page, open the Edit menu and choose Select, and then choose either Sentence, Paragraph, or Page.

To select a block of text, drag over the text (click and hold the left mouse button to drag). Or press **Alt+F4**, and use the cursor movement keys to highlight the text:

To block this text	Press this
One character at a time	← or →
One line at a time	↑ or ↓
One word at a time	CTRL + ← or →
One paragraph at a time	CTRL + ↑ or ↓
One page at a time	PG UP or PG DN

COPYING OR MOVING TEXT BETWEEN DOCUMENTS

Exercise

Open two documents to practice moving text between them. (If you need help, see "Opening an Existing Document" earlier in this part.)

1 Open two documents.

2 Click on the Window menu, or press **Alt+W**. Click on Tile, or press **T**.

3 Select some text in the first document to practice moving.

4 Click on the Edit menu, or press **Alt+E**.

5 Click on Cut, or press **T**.

6 Click in the other document window, or press **Shift+F3**.

7 Move the cursor to where you would like to place the text.

8 Click on Edit, or press **Alt+E**. Click on Paste, or press **P**.

PREVIEWING A DOCUMENT BEFORE YOU PRINT IT

Why Preview a Document?

If you work in Graphics Mode, your document will appear on-screen as it will print, except for headers, footers, and footnotes that don't appear at all. To see how the entire page will look when printed (complete with headers and footers in place), use File Print Preview.

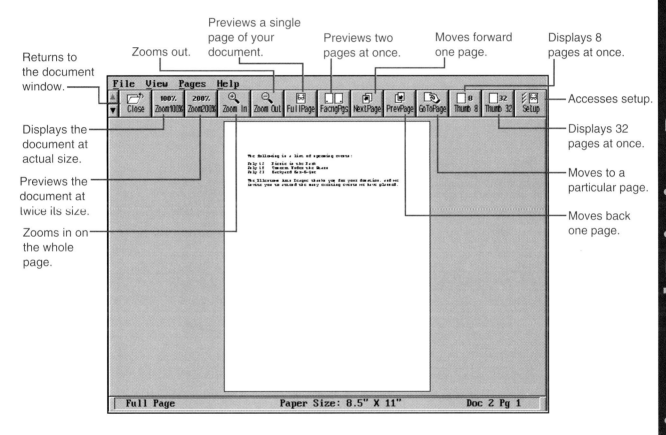

Previews a single page of your document.

Zooms out.

Previews two pages at once.

Moves forward one page.

Displays 8 pages at once.

Returns to the document window.

Displays the document at actual size.

Previews the document at twice its size.

Zooms in on the whole page.

Accesses setup.

Displays 32 pages at once.

Moves to a particular page.

Moves back one page.

TIP

Preview a document quickly by clicking on the **Print Preview** button on the Button Bar or pressing **Shift+F7**.

TIP

Print Preview isn't perfect; depending on the font you are using, there may be small differences between what you see on-screen and the way that the text looks when printed.

PREVIEWING A DOCUMENT BEFORE YOU PRINT IT

Previewing a Document Before You Print It

1 Click on the File menu, or press **Alt+F**.

2 Click on Print Preview, or press **V**.

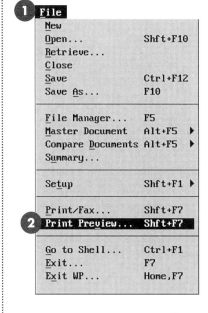

3 Select any preview options you want.

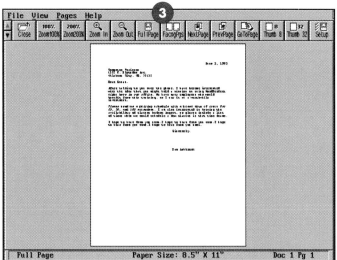

QUICK REFRESHER

To move around the Print Preview window when the entire page is not displayed, you can press **Page Up** or **Page Down**, or use the scroll bars.

Click on the up arrow to see the top of the page.

Click on the down arrow to see the bottom of the page.

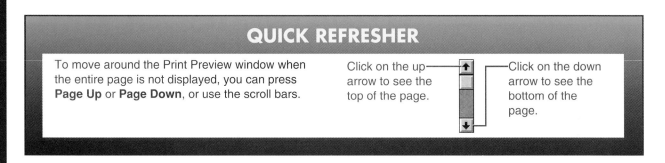

PRINTING A DOCUMENT

When Should You Print a Document?

You can print your document at any time, but because printing a document (especially a long one) can be time consuming, you'll want to preview the document before you print. That way, you can make sure that everything is the way you want it *before you print*.

When you're ready to print, use the **File Print** command. You have many print options from which you can choose, as shown in this figure. If you don't want to change any of the standard printing options, you don't have to; simply select the **Print** button as explained in the steps that follow.

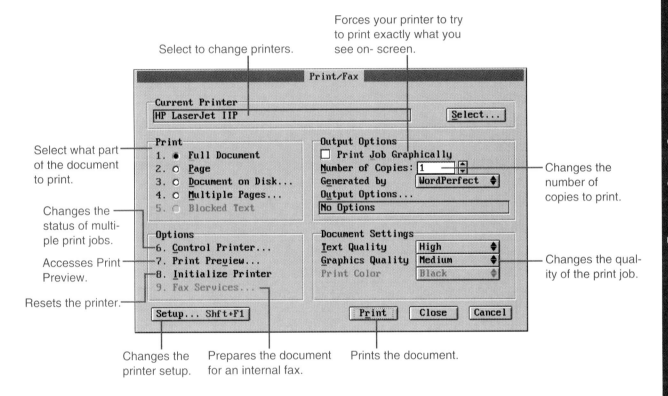

Forces your printer to try to print exactly what you see on- screen.

Select to change printers.

Select what part of the document to print.

Changes the status of multiple print jobs.

Accesses Print Preview.

Resets the printer.

Changes the number of copies to print.

Changes the quality of the print job.

Changes the printer setup.

Prepares the document for an internal fax.

Prints the document.

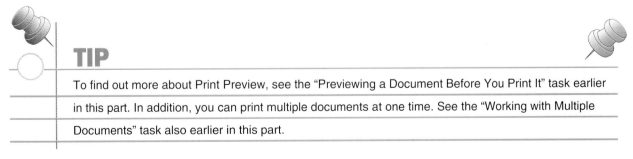

TIP

To find out more about Print Preview, see the "Previewing a Document Before You Print It" task earlier in this part. In addition, you can print multiple documents at one time. See the "Working with Multiple Documents" task also earlier in this part.

Opening, Saving, and Printing Documents

PRINTING A DOCUMENT

Printing a Document

1 Click on the File menu, or press **Alt+F**.

2 Click on **Print/Fax**, or press **P**.

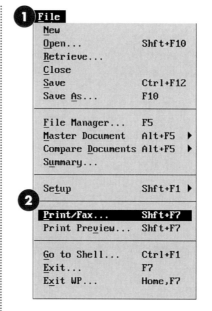

3 Change print options, if necessary.

4 Click on **Print**, or press **Enter**.

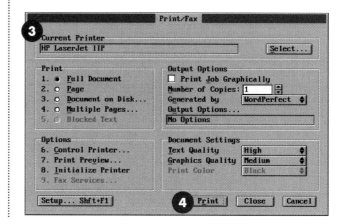

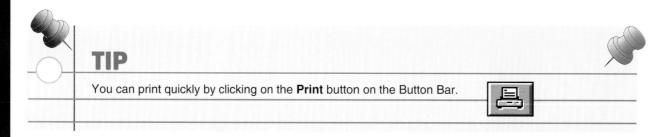

TIP

You can print quickly by clicking on the **Print** button on the Button Bar.

PART 4

Changing the Way Your Document Looks

In this part, you'll learn how to change the way text looks by adding bold or underline. You will also learn how to change the way paragraphs look: to create centered headings, indented paragraphs, a right-justified address, and bulleted or numbered lists. In addition, you'll learn how to make changes that affect the entire document: changing the paper size, orientation, and page margins.

- Revealing Formatting Codes
- Displaying and Using the Ribbon
- Formatting Characters
- Formatting Paragraphs
- Changing Paragraph Indentation
- Setting Page Margins
- Setting Tabs
- Changing Page Size and Orientation
- Adding Page Numbers
- Adding a Header or a Footer

REVEALING FORMATTING CODES

Why Reveal Codes?

Hiding behind the *formatting* you see on-screen are WordPerfect's formatting codes. For example, when you underline some text, two codes are inserted into your document: an "underline on" code is placed at the front of the underlined text, and an "underline off" code is placed at the end. If the "underline off" code is accidentally deleted, then the remaining text in your document is underlined. When you reveal the formatting codes, you can see these codes on screen and edit them, if necessary.

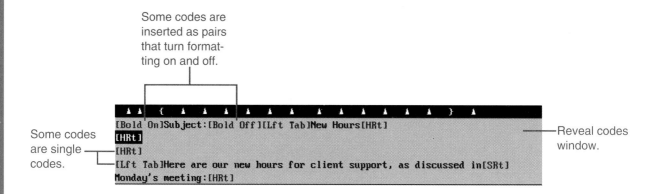

Some codes are inserted as pairs that turn formatting on and off.

Some codes are single codes.

Reveal codes window.

LEARNING THE LINGO

Formatting: The process of changing the look of a character (to make text look bold, underlined, and slightly bigger, for example) or a paragraph (by centering the paragraph between the margins or by adding an automatic indentation for the first line, for example).

Revealing Formatting Codes

1 Click on the View menu, or press **Alt+V**.

2 Click on Reveal Codes, or press **C**.

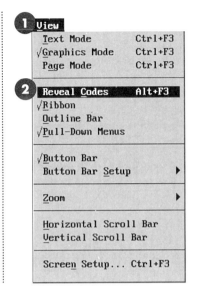

TIP

You can toggle between displaying the formatting codes and hiding them by pressing **Alt+F3** or **F11**.

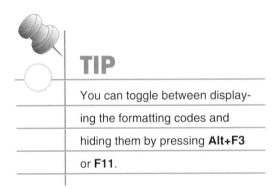

TIP

If you've inserted too many formatting codes, you can delete them by highlighting the codes in the Reveal Codes window and pressing **Delete**.

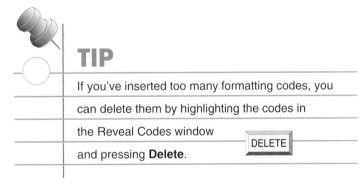

Changing the Way Your Document Looks

DISPLAYING AND USING THE RIBBON

Why Use the Ribbon?

For those of you who use a mouse, the Ribbon provides quick access to common formatting commands, such as changing the *font* or *point size* of the text. The Ribbon appears under the menu bar when displayed. To use the Ribbon, select the text you want to format, and then click on the appropriate option on the Ribbon. Initially, the Ribbon is not displayed. In this task, you'll learn how to turn the Ribbon on (display it) and some tips for using the Ribbon.

Click here to select a style for the selected paragraph.

Click here to change the paragraph justification.

Click here to change the size of text.

Click here to change your view of the document.

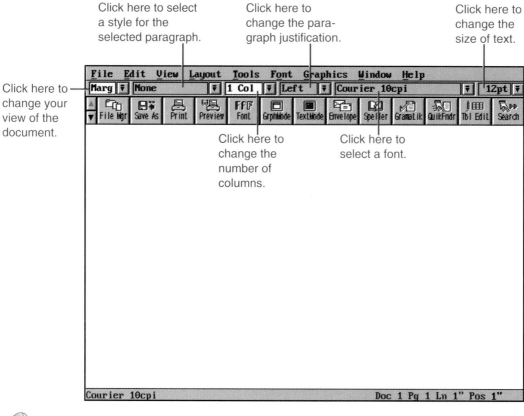

Click here to change the number of columns.

Click here to select a font.

Displaying the Ribbon

1 Click on the **View** menu, or press **Alt+V**.

2 Click on **R**ibbon, or press **R**.

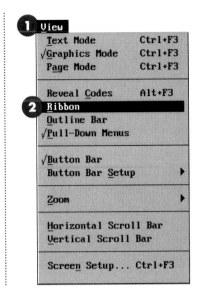

QUICK REFRESHER

To open a drop-down list box on the Ribbon, click on the arrow to the right of the list box. Once a box is open, click on an option to select it.

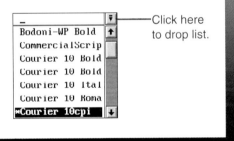

Click here to drop list.

Changing the Way Your Document Looks

FORMATTING CHARACTERS

Why Format Characters?

Formatting changes the way text looks. For example, to emphasize a word or a heading, you can increase the *point size* of text or add bold or italic (or bold *and* italic, if you wish). In addition, you can change the mood of a document (from serious to informal) by changing the *font*.

Change the formatting of text before you type it, or select the existing text you want to change, and then format it. If you turn on a text enhancement *before you enter text*, then you have to turn it off when you're finished. When you turn off the text enhancement, you will return to normal text. For example, you can "turn on bold," type a heading, "turn off bold," and return to normal text.

Select to add text enhancements.

Select to choose a different font.

Select to change the size of text.

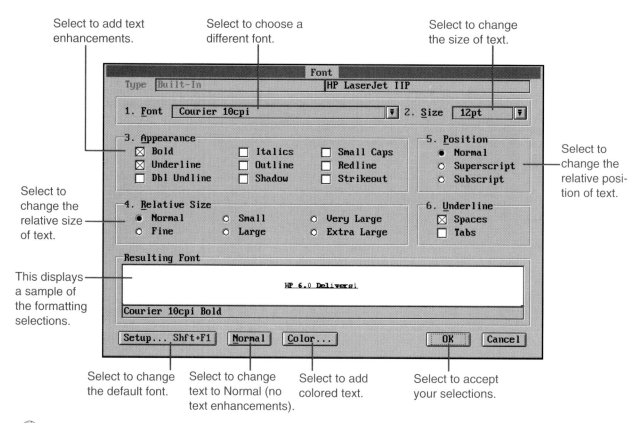

Select to change the relative position of text.

Select to change the relative size of text.

This displays a sample of the formatting selections.

Select to change the default font.

Select to change text to Normal (no text enhancements).

Select to add colored text.

Select to accept your selections.

TIP

To change text quickly, press **Ctrl+F8**	Bold	**F6**
to access the Font dialog box, or use one	Underline	**F8**
of these shortkeys:	Italics	**Ctrl+I**

Formatting Characters

1 If you want to change existing text, select it now.

1 The following is a list of upcoming events:

2 Click on the Font menu, or press **Alt+O**.

3 Click on Font, or press **O**.

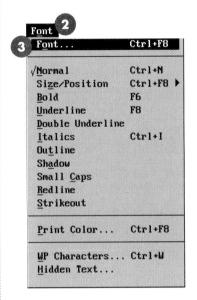

```
Font  2
3  Font...              Ctrl+F8

  √Normal               Ctrl+N
   Size/Position        Ctrl+F8 ▶
   Bold                 F6
   Underline            F8
   Double Underline
   Italics              Ctrl+I
   Outline
   Shadow
   Small Caps
   Redline
   Strikeout

   Print Color...       Ctrl+F8

   WP Characters...     Ctrl+W
   Hidden Text...
```

4 Select the text enhancements you want.

5 Click on **OK**, or press **Enter**.

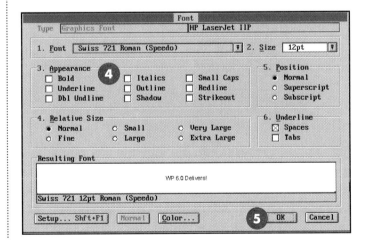

```
                              Font
 Type  Graphics Font                    HP LaserJet IIP

 1. Font  Swiss 721 Roman (Speedo)      ▼  2. Size  12pt   ▼

 3. Appearance                                   5. Position
    □ Bold      4   □ Italics    □ Small Caps       ● Normal
    □ Underline      □ Outline    □ Redline          ○ Superscript
    □ Dbl Undline    □ Shadow     □ Strikeout        ○ Subscript

 4. Relative Size                                6. Underline
    ● Normal    ○ Small     ○ Very Large           ⊠ Spaces
    ○ Fine      ○ Large     ○ Extra Large          □ Tabs

 Resulting Font

                    WP 6.0 Delivers!

 Swiss 721 12pt Roman (Speedo)

 Setup... Shft+F1   Normal   Color...        5   OK    Cancel
```

TIP

If you are entering text with particular text enhancements (such as bold text), remember to repeat the formatting steps after the text to return to normal.

Changing the Way Your Document Looks

FORMATTING CHARACTERS

Exercise

Type in the text shown here, and then follow the instructions to format the text.

1 Select the heading, **Get a Move On!**.

2 Press **F6** to make it bold.

3 Select the heading again.

4 Click on the Ribbon to open the point size drop-down list.

5 Select a large point size, such as 24.

> Get a Move On!
>
> Everyone must pack by 5:00 Friday. The movers will come in over the weekend and move us to our new offices. Make sure you:

LEARNING THE LINGO

Font: Any set of characters that share the same *typeface* (style or design). Fonts convey the mood and style of a document. Technically, font describes the combination of the *typeface* and the *point size* of a character, as in Times Roman 12-point, but in common usage, the font describes only a character's style or typeface.

Point size: The type size of a particular character. There are 72 points in an inch. Font families usually have only certain point sizes available; if you need larger or smaller letters than your font offers, switch to a different font.

QUICK REFRESHER

You can change the font or point size of text by using the appropriate drop-down list on the Ribbon.

Courier 10cpi ▼ 12pt ▼

You can also access the Font dialog box by clicking on the **Font** button on the Button Bar.

FFF

FORMATTING PARAGRAPHS

Why Format Paragraphs?

Formatting paragraphs changes the way they look. For example, you can center a heading or right *justify* an address. With the Layout Line command whose dialog box is shown in the figure, you can also change from single to double line spacing, adjust the amount of hyphenation in a paragraph, and add a border. You can select a paragraph first, and then change its formatting. This method affects only the paragraphs you select. As an alternative, you can place the cursor in a paragraph and then change the formatting; using this method, you affect all the paragraphs that follow.

In addition to the formatting changes listed here, you can adjust tab settings, paper size and orientation, and both paragraph and page margins within a document. You'll learn how to change these settings in later tasks in this part.

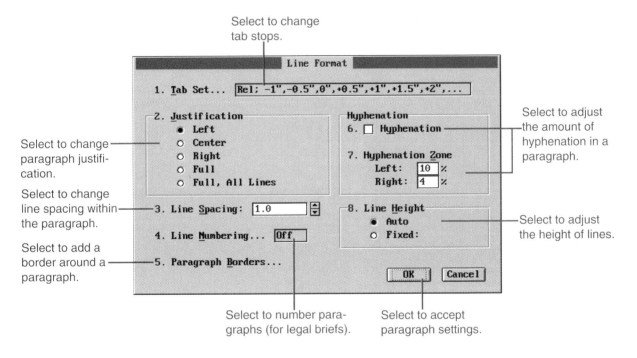

Select to change tab stops.

Select to change paragraph justification.

Select to change line spacing within the paragraph.

Select to add a border around a paragraph.

Select to adjust the amount of hyphenation in a paragraph.

Select to adjust the height of lines.

Select to number paragraphs (for legal briefs).

Select to accept paragraph settings.

TIP

For more information on changing tab settings, see the "Setting Tabs" task later in this part.

TIP

To change paragraph formatting quickly, move to the paragraph whose formatting you wish to change, then press **Shift+F8**. Press **1** to move to the Line Format dialog box.

Formatting Paragraphs

1 Move the cursor to the first paragraph whose formatting you wish to change. If you wish to change only certain paragraphs (and not all the preceding paragraphs) select them first.

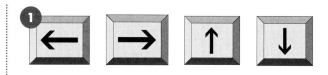

2 Click on the **L**ayout menu, or press **Alt+L**.

3 Click on **L**ine, or press **L**.

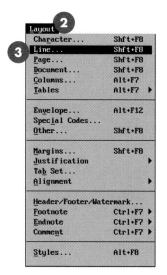

4 Select the paragraph settings you want to change.

5 Click on **OK**, or press **Enter**.

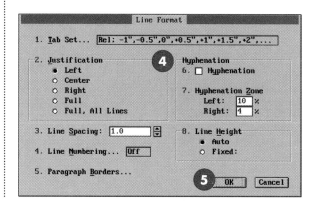

LEARNING THE LINGO

Justification: Controls how the text in a paragraph is placed between the left and right margins. You can left justify (text is even along the left edge of the paragraph), right justify (text is even along the right edge of the paragraph), center, or fully justify (text is even along both edges of the paragraph).

Exercise

Type the text shown here, and then follow these instructions to format the paragraphs.

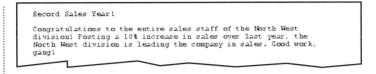

Record Sales Year!

Congratulations to the entire sales staff of the North West division! Posting a 10% increase in sales over last year, the North West division is leading the company in sales. Good work, gang!

1 Select the heading, **Record Sales Year!**.

2 Click on the Layout menu, or press **Alt+L**.

3 Click on Line, or press **L**.

4 Under Justification, select Center to center the heading.

5 Select Paragraph Borders.

6 Select Border Style.

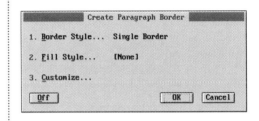

Create Paragraph Border

1. Border Style...   Single Border

2. Fill Style...   [None]

3. Customize...

[Off]   [OK] [Cancel]

7 Select **Double Border**.

8 Click on **OK**, or press **Enter** to return to the Line Format dialog box.

9 Click on **OK**, or press **Enter** again to return to the document.

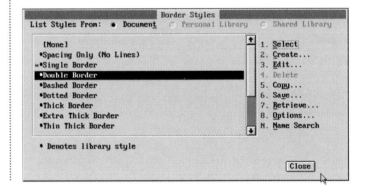

Border Styles

List Styles From: ● Document   ○ Personal Library   ○ Shared Library

[None]
*●Spacing Only (No Lines)
*●Single Border
●Double Border
●Dashed Border
●Dotted Border
●Thick Border
●Extra Thick Border
●Thin Thick Border

1. Select
2. Create...
3. Edit...
4. Delete
5. Copy...
6. Save...
7. Retrieve...
8. Options...
N. Name Search

● Denotes library style

[Close]

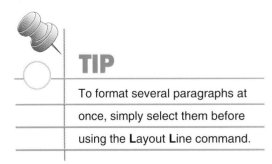

TIP

To format several paragraphs at once, simply select them before using the Layout Line command.

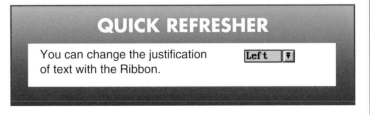

QUICK REFRESHER

You can change the justification of text with the Ribbon.

Left ▼

Changing the Way Your Document Looks

CHANGING PARAGRAPH INDENTATION

Why Change Indentation?

You use indentation to adjust the distance between margins and the edges of individual paragraphs. Indentation is different than just pressing Tab at the beginning of a paragraph. Indentation (which WordPerfect sometimes refers to as *alignment*) moves the lines in a paragraph an extra distance in from the margins. For example, by using the **Layout Margins** command as shown in the figure, you can add a left indent to a paragraph to set off important information by moving all the lines in that paragraph an extra distance from the left margin. You can, of course, define a first line indent only and avoid having to press Tab to indent your paragraphs. In addition, you can create a *hanging indent* for bulleted or numbered lists.

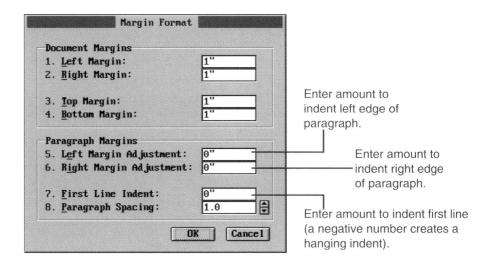

Enter amount to indent left edge of paragraph.

Enter amount to indent right edge of paragraph.

Enter amount to indent first line (a negative number creates a hanging indent).

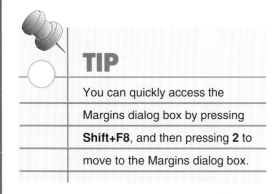

TIP

You can quickly access the Margins dialog box by pressing **Shift+F8**, and then pressing **2** to move to the Margins dialog box.

LEARNING THE LINGO

Hanging indent: A special kind of indent where the first line of a paragraph hangs closer to the left margin than the rest of the lines in the paragraph. Hanging indents are typically used for bulleted or numbered lists.

Indent: The amount of distance from the page margins to the edges of your paragraph. Sometimes referred to as "changing the alignment" of a paragraph.

Margin: An area on the left and right sides of a page that is usually left blank. Text flows between the margins of a page.

Changing Paragraph Indentation

1 Place the insertion point at the beginning of the paragraph you want to change by pressing **Ctrl+up arrow**.

2 Click on the Layout menu, or press **Alt+L**.

3 Click Margins, or press **M**.

1 CTRL + ↑

2 Layout

Character...	Shft+F8
Line...	Shft+F8
Page...	Shft+F8
Document...	Shft+F8
Columns...	Alt+F7
Tables	Alt+F7 ▶
Envelope...	Alt+F12
Special Codes...	
Other...	Shft+F8
3 Margins...	Shft+F8
Justification	▶
Tab Set...	
Alignment	▶
Header/Footer/Watermark...	
Footnote	Ctrl+F7 ▶
Endnote	Ctrl+F7 ▶
Comment	Ctrl+F7 ▶
Styles...	Alt+F8

4 Enter the amounts to indent.

5 Click on **OK**, or press **Enter**.

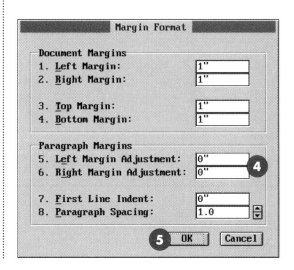

Margin Format

Document Margins
1. Left Margin: `1"`
2. Right Margin: `1"`

3. Top Margin: `1"`
4. Bottom Margin: `1"`

Paragraph Margins
5. Left Margin Adjustment: `0"`
6. Right Margin Adjustment: `0"` **4**

7. First Line Indent: `0"`
8. Paragraph Spacing: `1.0`

5 OK   Cancel

Changing the Way Your Document Looks

CHANGING PARAGRAPH INDENTATION

Exercise

Type the text shown here, and then change the indentation by following these instructions.

1 Place the insertion point at the beginning of the first paragraph.

2 Click on the **Layout** menu, or press **Alt+L**.

3 Click **Margins**, or press **M**.

4 Enter the amount to indent: First Line = .5.

5 Click on **OK**.

6 Select all of the bulleted lines.

7 Click on the **Layout** menu, or press **Alt+L**.

8 Click on **Margins**, or press **M**.

9 Enter the amounts to indent: Left = 1 First Line = −.5.

```
Get a Move On!

Everyone must pack by 5:00 Friday. The movers will come in over
the weekend and move us to our new offices. Make sure you:

o    Pack the contents of your desk, including the top drawer.

o    Pack all file cabinets.

o    Do not pack bookcases - the movers will take care of that!

o    Label each box with your name and extension.
```

TIP

Like paragraph formatting, changing indentation affects all paragraphs that follow.

Another thing to remember when indenting a paragraph: make sure you always place the cursor at the beginning of the paragraph before you indent. Otherwise, the indent will be inserted into the middle of the paragraph, at the current cursor location.

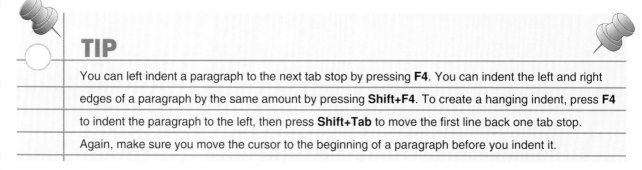

TIP

You can left indent a paragraph to the next tab stop by pressing **F4**. You can indent the left and right edges of a paragraph by the same amount by pressing **Shift+F4**. To create a hanging indent, press **F4** to indent the paragraph to the left, then press **Shift+Tab** to move the first line back one tab stop. Again, make sure you move the cursor to the beginning of a paragraph before you indent it.

SETTING PAGE MARGINS

Why Set Page Margins?

Page margins control the amount of space between the edge of the page and the text of your document. You can further control the amount of space between the edge of the page and a paragraph by adding an indent. See the "Changing Paragraph Indentation" task earlier in this part.

Using the **Layout/Margins** command as shown in the figure, you can adjust the left, right, top, and bottom margins of the entire document or individual pages. (To change page margins for selected pages, change them on the first page you wish, and then change the margins back to their original settings later in your document.) When you change the page margins within a document, all subsequent pages are affected.

Enter left margin amount.

Enter right margin amount.

Enter the amount for top margin.

Enter amount for bottom margin.

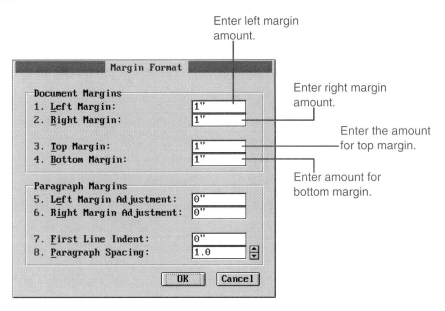

TIP

You can change page margins quickly by pressing **Shift+F8**, and then press **3** to move to the Margins dialog box.

TIP

To center the text between the top and bottom margins, use the **Layout Page** command, then click on **C**enter Current Page or Center **P**ages.

Changing the Way Your Document Looks

SETTING PAGE MARGINS

Setting Page Margins

1 Move to the first page in the document where you want to change the page margins. To move to the top of the document, press **Home+Home+up arrow**.

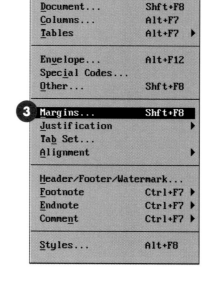

2 Click on the Layout menu, or press **Alt+L**.

3 Click on **Margins**, or press **M**.

4 Enter the new margin settings.

5 Click on **OK**, or press **Enter**.

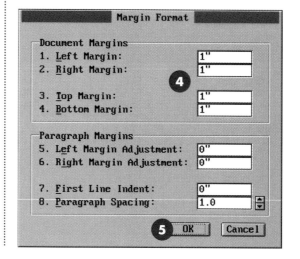

Why Set Tabs?

WordPerfect has default tabs set every .5" beginning 1/2" from the left margin. If you want to move to the first tab setting, simply press **Tab**. To move backward to a previous tab setting, press **Shift+Tab**. If the default settings are fine, you don't need to change the tab settings. However, if you are creating a small list, such as a listing of salespeople and their gross sales this month, the default tab settings may not be adequate. For example, the column of gross sales should use a *decimal tab* so that the dollar amounts line up properly. Changing the tab settings allows you to change the type of tab.

Using the **L**ayout **T**ab command as shown in the figure, you can specify the normal *left-aligned tab* (aligns characters on the left), *right-aligned tab* (aligns characters on the right), *decimal tab* (aligns numbers by the decimal point), or *center tab* (aligns headings above columns). You can also add a *leader* between tabs. In any case, when you change tab settings, they are effective from that point forward (the current cursor position); the new settings do not affect previous pages in the document.

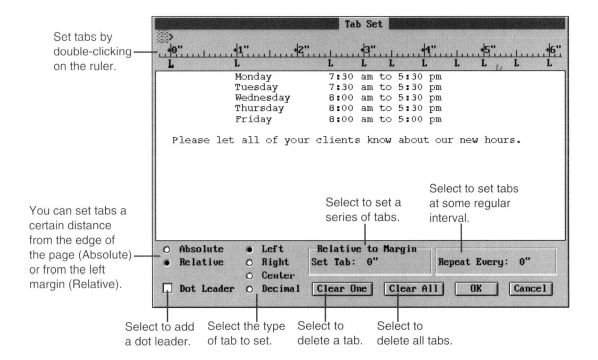

Set tabs by double-clicking on the ruler.

You can set tabs a certain distance from the edge of the page (Absolute) or from the left margin (Relative).

Select to set a series of tabs.

Select to set tabs at some regular interval.

Select to add a dot leader.

Select the type of tab to set.

Select to delete a tab.

Select to delete all tabs.

Changing the Way Your Document Looks

Setting Tabs

1 Move to the place in the document where you want to change the tab settings. To move to the top of the document, press **Home+Home+up arrow**.

2 Click on the **Layout** menu, or press **Alt+L**.

3 Click on Tab Set, or press **T**.

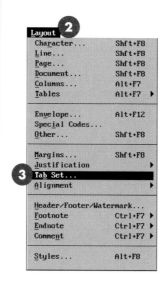

4 Select the tab settings you want.

5 Clear any unnecessary tabs.

6 Set the tabs you want by double-clicking on the ruler (see the Tip for additional methods you can use to set tabs).

7 Click on **OK**, or press **Enter** to accept tab settings.

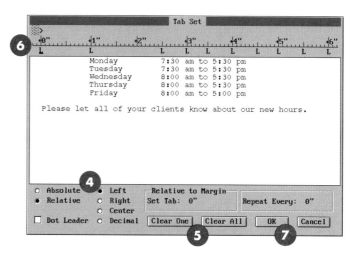

LEARNING THE LINGO

Leader: Dots that fill the spaces between tab positions in a columnar list.

Tab: A keystroke that moves the cursor to a specified point. Used to align columns of text.

Exercise

Type the text shown here. When you enter the table, press **Tab** between the name of the division and each number. Then follow these steps to change the tab settings.

1 Move the insertion point to the first line under the heading.

2 Click on the **Layout** menu, or press **Alt+L**.

3 Click on Tab Set, or press **T**.

4 Select **Clear All**.

5 Click on the ruler at 1.5, and then **Left**.

6 Click on the ruler at 3.5, and then click on **Decimal**.

7 Click on the ruler at 5, and then click on **Decimal**.

8 Click on **OK**, or press **Enter**.

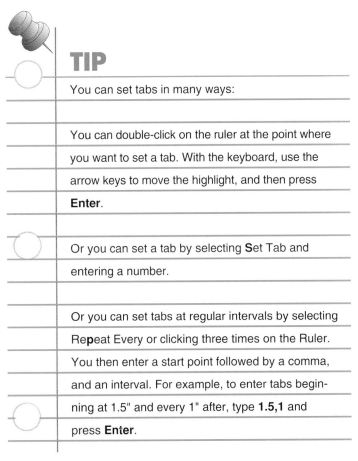

```
Record Sales Year!

Congratulations to the entire sales staff of the North West
division! Posting a 10% increase in sales over last year, the
North West division is leading the company in sales. Good work.
gang!

Here's how we all stack up:

North West      112,134.00      113,978.00
South West      111,987.00      110,123.00
South East       99,876.00 98,786.00
North East       88,967.00 96,879.00
```

TIP

Within the Tab Set dialog box, you can delete the tabs from the current position to the end by pressing **Ctrl+End**. To delete all the tabs, select Clear **A**ll.

TIP

You can set tabs in many ways:

You can double-click on the ruler at the point where you want to set a tab. With the keyboard, use the arrow keys to move the highlight, and then press **Enter**.

Or you can set a tab by selecting **S**et Tab and entering a number.

Or you can set tabs at regular intervals by selecting Re**p**eat Every or clicking three times on the Ruler. You then enter a start point followed by a comma, and an interval. For example, to enter tabs beginning at 1.5" and every 1" after, type **1.5,1** and press **Enter**.

Changing the Way Your Document Looks

CHANGING PAGE SIZE AND ORIENTATION

Why Change Page Size or Orientation?

If you want to print on any other size paper than 8 1/2" x 11", such as 8 1/2" x 14", you'll need to change the paper size. *Orientation*, on the other hand, has nothing to do with the size of the paper on which you're printing, but with the direction in which your document is printed on the paper size you select.

When you use the Layout Page command as shown in the figure, you can change both the size and the orientation of the paper you are using to print. When you make a change to the current paper size or orientation, all subsequent pages are affected.

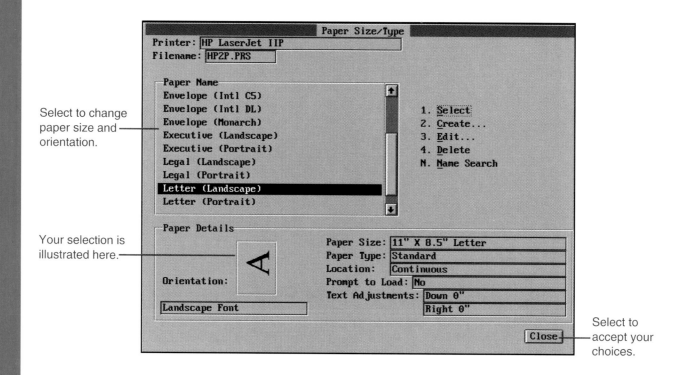

Select to change paper size and orientation.

Your selection is illustrated here.

Select to accept your choices.

LEARNING THE LINGO

Portrait orientation: Your document is positioned so that it is longer than it is wide, as in 8 1/2" x 11". This is the normal orientation of most documents.

Landscape orientation: Your document is positioned so that it is wider than it is long, as in 11" x 8 1/2".

Changing Page Size and Orientation

1 Move to the page within your document where you want to change the page size or orientation. To move to the top of the document, press **Home+Home+up arrow**.

2 Click on the Layout menu, or press **Alt+L**.

3 Click on **P**age, or press **P**.

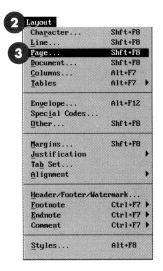

4 Click on Paper **S**ize/Type, or press **S**.

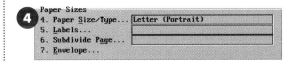

5 Select a paper size and orientation by double-clicking on it, or highlighting it and pressing **S** for Select.

6 Click on **OK**, or press **Enter**.

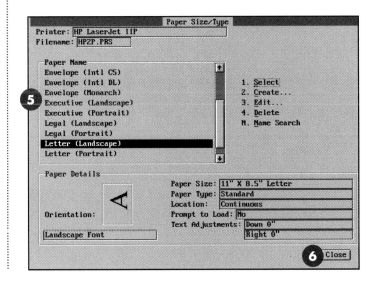

Changing the Way Your Document Looks

ADDING PAGE NUMBERS

Why Should You Add Page Numbers?

Page numbers can help readers keep track of where they are within a document, if the document is more than a few pages long. Page numbers can also help you keep the pages of your documents in order during copying and distribution.

You can add page numbers to your document in several ways: within a *header*, a *footer*, or by themselves. (See the "Adding Headers and Footers" task in this part.) Also, you can change the starting page number and the numbering system (from 1, 2, 3 to a, b, c, for example). In any case, page numbering begins on the current page and continues to the end of the document (unless you turn it off by repeating the steps listed here and choosing None under Page Number **P**osition).

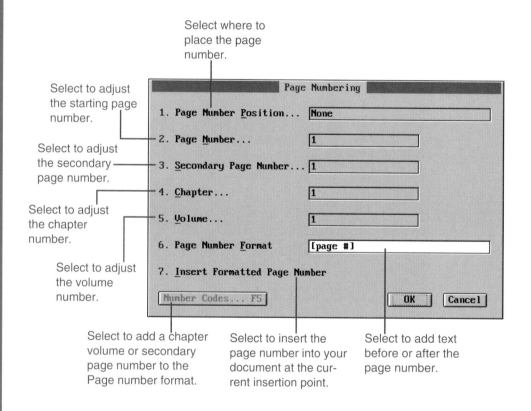

Select where to place the page number.

Select to adjust the starting page number.

Select to adjust the secondary page number.

Select to adjust the chapter number.

Select to adjust the volume number.

Select to add a chapter volume or secondary page number to the Page number format.

Select to insert the page number into your document at the current insertion point.

Select to add text before or after the page number.

(Dialog box labeled "Page Numbering")
1. Page Number **P**osition... None
2. Page **N**umber... 1
3. **S**econdary Page Number... 1
4. **C**hapter... 1
5. **V**olume... 1
6. Page Number **F**ormat [page #]
7. **I**nsert Formatted Page Number

Number Codes... F5   OK   Cancel

LEARNING THE LINGO

Header: Text that can be made to appear at the top of every page in a document.

Footer: Text that can be made to appear at the bottom of every page in a document.

Adding Page Numbers

1 Move to where you want to begin adding page numbers. To move to the top of the document, press **Home+Home+up arrow**.

2 Click on the **L**ayout menu, or press **Alt+L**.

3 Click on **P**age, or press **P**.

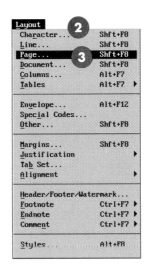

4 Click on Page **N**umbering, or press **N**.

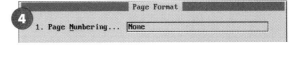

5 Click on Page Number **P**osition or press **P.**

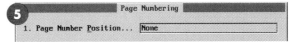

TIP

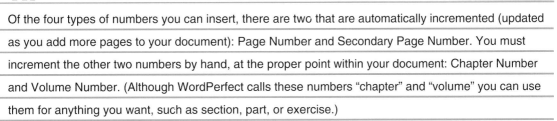

Of the four types of numbers you can insert, there are two that are automatically incremented (updated as you add more pages to your document): Page Number and Secondary Page Number. You must increment the other two numbers by hand, at the proper point within your document: Chapter Number and Volume Number. (Although WordPerfect calls these numbers "chapter" and "volume" you can use them for anything you want, such as section, part, or exercise.)

ADDING PAGE NUMBERS

6 Select where to place the page number on the page.

7 Click on **OK**, or press **Enter**.

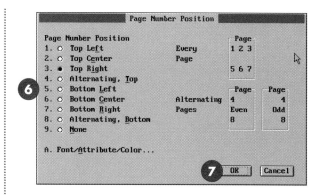

8 You can change the starting page number or the number type in the Page **N**umber box.

9 You can add text before or after the page number in the Page Number **F**ormat box.

10 If you want to add a chapter, volume, or secondary page number, click here.

11 Click on **OK**, or press **Enter**.

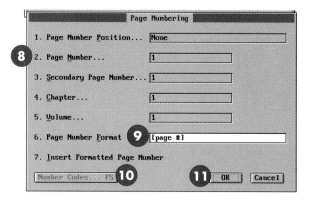

TIP

If you are using chapter or volume number, you must remember to manually increment the number at the appropriate point within your document. Move to the first page of the new chapter or volume, and then follow these instructions. After step 7, click on **C**hapter or **V**olume, and then click on Increment. Continue with step 8.

ADDING A HEADER OR A FOOTER

Why Add a Header or a Footer?

A *header* is text that can be repeated at the top of every page, and a *footer* is text that can be repeated at the bottom of every page. For example, you can create a header or footer that contains the title of your report. You can even create a different header or footer for odd versus even pages (look at the headers in this book). In addition, you can add page numbers to your header or footer.

TIP

While entering your header or footer, you can format text (add bold or italics or change the font, for example) or add page numbers. Just open the appropriate menu and follow the instructions given in previous tasks.

Adding a Header or a Footer

1 Click on the Layout menu, or press **Alt+L**.

2 Click on Header/Footer/Watermark, or press **H**.

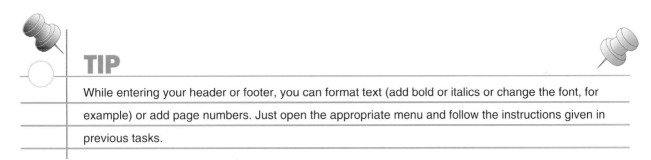

QUICK REFRESHER

To view a completed header or footer, click on the **Print Preview** button on the Button Bar.

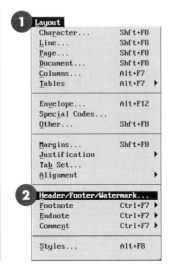

ADDING A HEADER OR A FOOTER

3 Click on **H**eader or **F**ooter, or press **H** or **F**.

4 Select either the first or second header or footer.

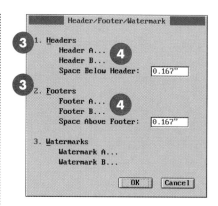

5 Click on **A**ll, **E**ven, or **O**dd, or press **A**, **V**, or **O**.

6 Click on **C**reate, or press C.

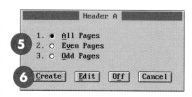

7 Enter or change your header or footer (you can use any of the commands that are marked as available to format your text or add page numbers).

8 Press **F7** to return to the Header/Footer/Watermark dialog box.

9 Click **OK** or press **Enter** to return to the document.

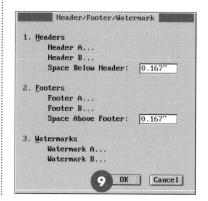

PART 5

Features That Make Life Easier

In this part, you'll learn how to perfect your documents. Thanks to spell checkers, grammar checkers, and the thesaurus, you can focus on what you're trying to say, rather than how you're saying it.

- Checking Your Spelling
- Using the Thesaurus
- Checking Your Grammar

CHECKING YOUR SPELLING

Why Use a Spelling Checker?

Using a spelling checker saves you time in proofreading your document. The spelling checker in WordPerfect not only checks for mistakes in spelling, but also for duplicate words (words used twice in a row). The spelling checker can also spot numbers in the middle of a word and irregularities in capitalization.

The spelling checker can check your entire document, a single page, a word, or a portion of the document starting at the current cursor position. When a possible misspelling is found, you have several choices. If a double word is found, or if you decide to look up a possible spelling for the word, you will see additional dialog boxes.

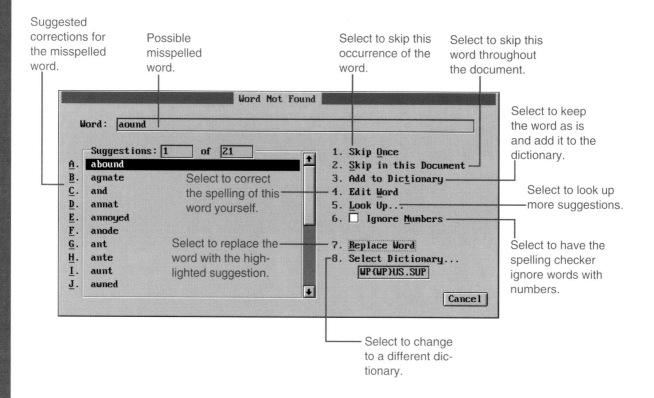

Suggested corrections for the misspelled word.

Possible misspelled word.

Select to skip this occurrence of the word.

Select to skip this word throughout the document.

Select to keep the word as is and add it to the dictionary.

Select to correct the spelling of this word yourself.

Select to look up more suggestions.

Select to replace the word with the highlighted suggestion.

Select to have the spelling checker ignore words with numbers.

Select to change to a different dictionary.

Word Not Found

Word: aound

Suggestions: 1 of 21
A. abound
B. agnate
C. and
D. annat
E. annoyed
F. anode
G. ant
H. ante
I. aunt
J. awned

1. Skip Once
2. Skip in this Document
3. Add to Dictionary
4. Edit Word
5. Look Up...
6. ☐ Ignore Numbers
7. Replace Word
8. Select Dictionary...
WP{WP}US.SUP

Cancel

Select to skip the duplicate word.

Select to edit the second word yourself.

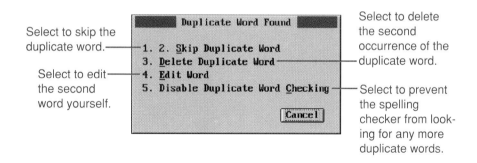

Select to delete the second occurrence of the duplicate word.

Select to prevent the spelling checker from looking for any more duplicate words.

Select a suggested replacement for the misspelled word.

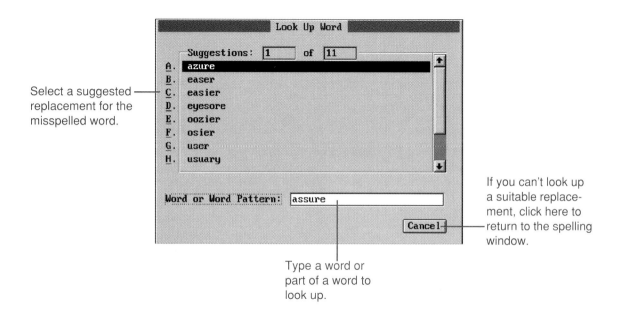

If you can't look up a suitable replacement, click here to return to the spelling window.

Type a word or part of a word to look up.

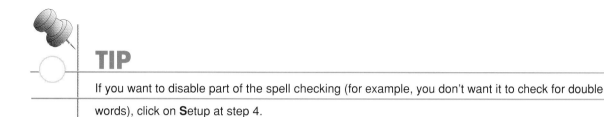

TIP

If you want to disable part of the spell checking (for example, you don't want it to check for double words), click on **S**etup at step 4.

Features That Make Life Easier

Checking Your Spelling

1 Click on the Tools menu, or press **Alt+T**.

2 Click on Writing Tools, or press **W**.

3 Click on Speller, or press **S**.

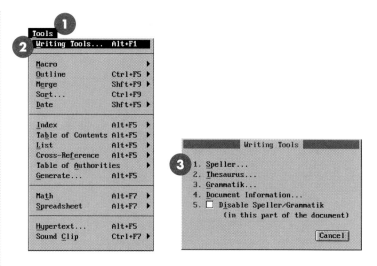

4 Select the part of the document to spell check.

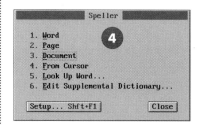

5 If a misspelled word is found, select an option such as Skip Once, Skip in this Document, Add to Dictionary, or Replace Word.

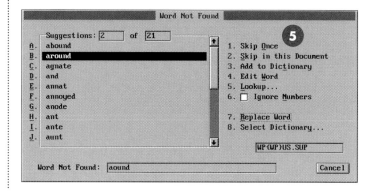

122

6 If you decide to edit the word yourself (by selecting Edit **W**ord in step 5), simply type your change and press **F7** when you are through. The spell check will continue.

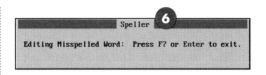

7 If you decide to look up a possible spelling (by selecting **Lookup** in step 5), type the word as you think it should be spelled and then either select the correction from the list or click on **Cancel** to return to the spelling window and try something else.

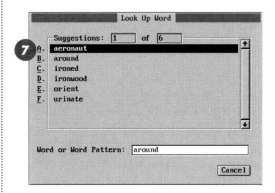

8 If a double word was found, select an appropriate option.

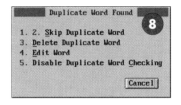

9 Spell check will continue until the entire section you indicated in step 4 has been checked. When the spell check is complete, click on **OK** or press **Enter**.

QUICK REFRESHER

To spell check a document quickly, click on the **Spelling** button on the Button Bar.

Features That Make Life Easier

USING THE THESAURUS

Why Use the Thesaurus?

Using a *thesaurus* to find synonyms and antonyms to commonly used words can add variety to a long letter or report. You can also use the thesaurus to find the "right word" to convey your exact meaning. Overuse of a thesaurus can make your writing seem stilted, so use the thesaurus with care. For example, although both sentences mean the same thing, it does not seem as natural to say, "Our sales for the fourth quarter were *consequential*." as it does to say, "Our sales for the fourth quarter were *great*."

You use the WordPerfect thesaurus on a word-by-word basis; move the insertion point to a word whose synonyms you want to look up, and then follow the steps in this task.

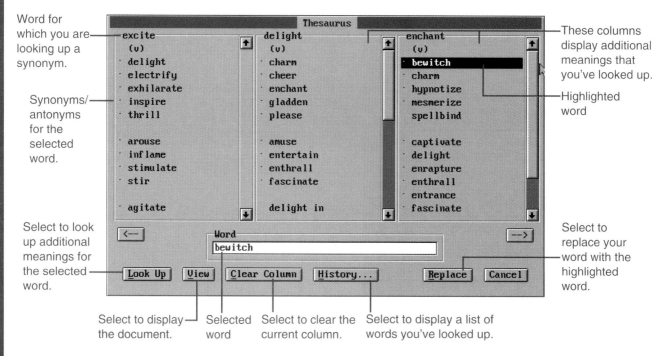

Word for which you are looking up a synonym.

Synonyms/antonyms for the selected word.

Select to look up additional meanings for the selected word.

Select to display the document.

Selected word

Select to clear the current column.

Select to display a list of words you've looked up.

These columns display additional meanings that you've looked up.

Highlighted word

Select to replace your word with the highlighted word.

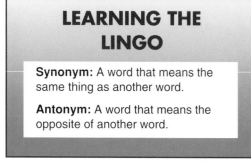

LEARNING THE LINGO

Synonym: A word that means the same thing as another word.

Antonym: A word that means the opposite of another word.

TIP

To quickly look up a synonym for a word in the Thesaurus dialog box, double-click on that word instead of using the **L**ook Up button.

Using the Thesaurus

1 Move the insertion point to the word you want to look up.

2 Click on the Tools menu, or press **Alt+T**.

3 Click on **Writing Tools**, or press **W**.

4 Click on Thesaurus, or press **T**.

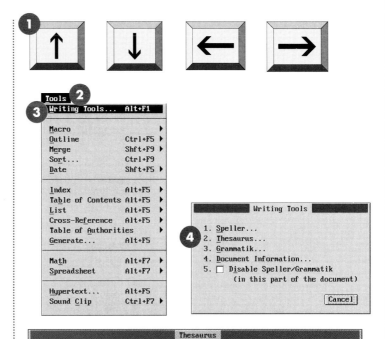

5 Select a replacement word from the list by clicking on it or using the arrow keys to highlight it.

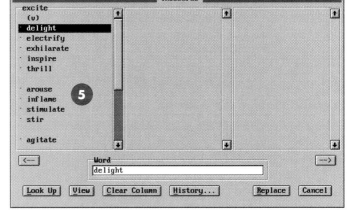

6 If you want to see additional synonyms for the highlighted word, click on **Look** Up and then press **Enter**.

7 When you've found a synonym to replace the word in your document, click on **Replace**, or press **R**.

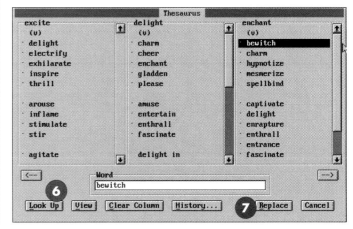

CHECKING YOUR GRAMMAR

Why Check Your Grammar?

As good as a spelling checker is, it is not perfect; it can't check for the improper use of a word. For example, a spelling checker will find nothing wrong with this sentence: "Continue with this procedure until your finished." The word **your** should be **you're** or **you are**, but since it's spelled correctly, the spelling checker won't flag it. To catch such mistakes in grammar, you should use the Grammatik grammar checker. After Grammatik is through checking your document, you can view statistics that let you judge the overall readability of your document. By the way, when you use Grammatik, it automatically checks your entire document (you cannot check part of a document as you can with the spell checker).

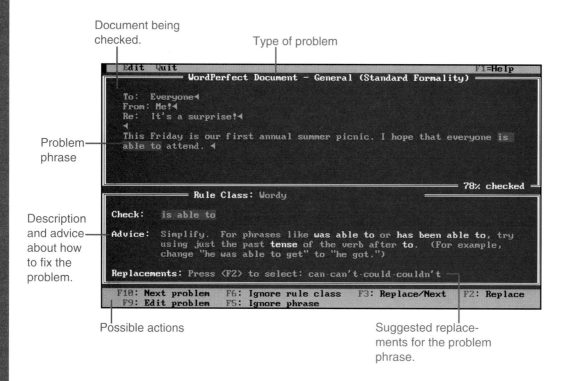

Document being checked.

Type of problem

Problem phrase

Description and advice about how to fix the problem.

Possible actions

Suggested replacements for the problem phrase.

LEARNING THE LINGO

Readability Index: A way of measuring the education level needed in order to easily understand the text in a given document by counting the average number of words per sentence and the average number of syllables per 100 words. (A good average is about 17 words per sentence and 147 syllables per 100 words.)

Readability
statistics

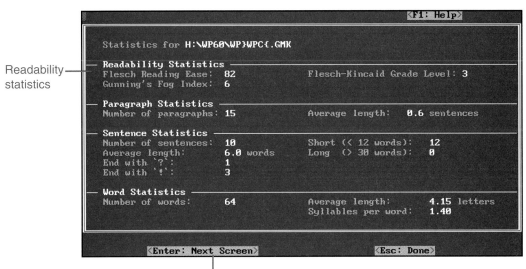

```
                                                        <F1: Help>
   Statistics for H:\WP60\WP}WPC{.GMK
  ─ Readability Statistics ─────────────────────────────────────
   Flesch Reading Ease:   82        Flesch-Kincaid Grade Level: 3
   Gunning's Fog Index:   6

  ─ Paragraph Statistics ──────────────────────────────────────
   Number of paragraphs: 15         Average length:    0.6 sentences

  ─ Sentence Statistics ───────────────────────────────────────
   Number of sentences:   10        Short (< 12 words):   12
   Average length:        6.0 words Long  (> 30 words):   0
   End with '?':          1
   End with '!':          3

  ─ Word Statistics ───────────────────────────────────────────
   Number of words:       64        Average length:     4.15 letters
                                    Syllables per word: 1.40

          <Enter: Next Screen>              <Esc: Done>
```

Press Enter to see
an explanation of
these statistics.

Explanation
of readability
statistics

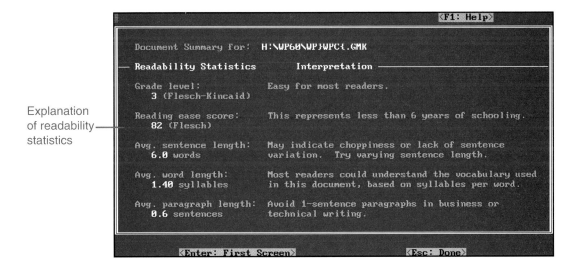

```
                                                        <F1: Help>
   Document Summary for:  H:\WP60\WP}WPC{.GMK

  ─ Readability Statistics        Interpretation ──────────────

   Grade level:             Easy for most readers.
     3 (Flesch-Kincaid)

   Reading ease score:      This represents less than 6 years of schooling.
     82 (Flesch)

   Avg. sentence length:    May indicate choppiness or lack of sentence
     6.0 words              variation.  Try varying sentence length.

   Avg. word length:        Most readers could understand the vocabulary used
     1.40 syllables         in this document, based on syllables per word.

   Avg. paragraph length:   Avoid 1-sentence paragraphs in business or
     0.6 sentences          technical writing.

          <Enter: First Screen>             <Esc: Done>
```

TIP

If you want to check the grammar of another document, use the **F**ile **O**pen command, and then press **I**
to begin the grammar check.

Features That Make Life Easier

CHECKING YOUR GRAMMAR

Checking Your Grammar

1 Click on the Tools menu, or press **Alt+T**.

2 Click on **Writing Tools**, or press **T**.

3 Click on **Grammatik**, or press **G**.

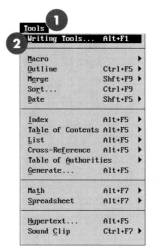

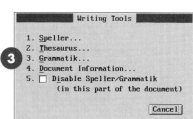

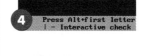

4 Press **I** to check the grammar of your current document.

5 If a problem phrase is found, take the appropriate action.

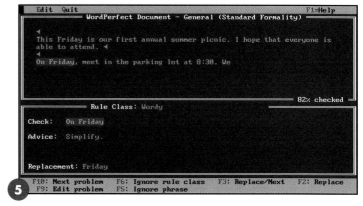

6 Press **F10** to look for the next problem.

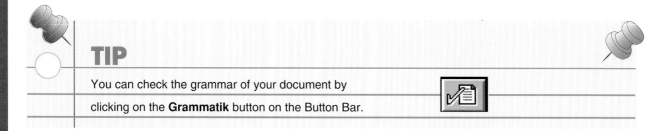

TIP

You can check the grammar of your document by clicking on the **Grammatik** button on the Button Bar.

128

7 Repeat steps 5 and 6, as necessary. When Grammatik is through checking your document, press **T** for a listing of statistics on readability.

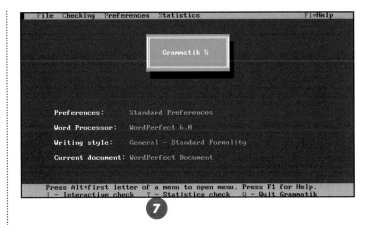

8 Press **Enter** to see an explanation of the readability statistics.

9 Press **Q** to quit Grammatik.

QUICK REFRESHER

If Grammatik finds an error, you have several choices:

F2 — Select a replacement phrase from a list of suggestions.

F3 — Display additional suggestions. Press **F7** when you are through

F5 — Ignore the problem phrase.

F6 — Ignore this type of problem for the rest of the document.

F9 — Edit the problem phrase yourself.

F10 — Continue to the next problem phrase.

Features That Make Life Easier

Glossary

active document   The document in which you are currently working. The active document contains the cursor (insertion point), and if more than one document window is being displayed on-screen, the active document's title bar appears darker than the other title bars.

alignment   Controls how the text in a paragraph is placed between the left and right margins. For example, you might have left-aligned or centered text. Also known as *justification*.

block   Any amount of selected text.

border   A line placed around a paragraph.

bulleted list   Similar to a numbered list. A bulleted list is a series of paragraphs with hanging indents, where the bullet (usually a dot or a check mark) is placed to the left of all the other lines in the paragraph. A bulleted list is often used to display a list of items or to summarize important points.

Button Bar   Presents the most common WordPerfect commands in an easy-to-access form. For example, clicking the Save button on the Button Bar saves your document.

click   To move the mouse pointer over an object or icon and press and release the mouse button once without moving the mouse.

Clipboard   A temporary storage area that holds text and graphics. The Cut and Copy commands put text or graphics on the Clipboard, erasing the Clipboard's previous contents. The Paste command copies Clipboard data to a document.

Close button   A small button located in the upper left-hand corner of a framed document that closes the document when it is clicked upon.

copying text   When you copy text, the selected text stays in its original location, and a copy of the selected text is placed where you indicate.

cursor   A blinking vertical line that moves across the page as you type. A cursor acts like the tip of your pencil; anything you type appears at the cursor. See also *insertion point*.

date code   An invisible code that represents the current date. This code is changed whenever you open a document for changes or print it.

date text   Text that WordPerfect can insert for you; use this instead of typing the date yourself. Date text is not updated as changes are made to the document.

dialog box   A dialog box is a special window or box that appears when the program requires additional information before a command can be executed.

directory   Because large hard disks can store thousands of files, you need directories to store related files. Think of your disk as a filing cabinet and think of each directory as a drawer in the filing cabinet. By keeping files in separate directories, you can easily locate and work with related files.

disk   A round, flat, magnetic storage unit. See *floppy disk* and *hard disk*.

document   Any work you create using a word processing program, such as a letter or a chapter of a book.

document backup   Saving your document in periodic intervals as you continue to work.

131

Document Summary   An optional part of a document where you can store information about the document's type, purpose, author, subject, and so on.

Document window   A window that frames the controls and information for the document file on which you are working. You can have multiple document windows open at one time.

double-click   To move the mouse pointer over an object or icon and press and release the mouse button twice in quick succession.

drag   To drag the mouse, first move the mouse to the starting position. Now click and hold the mouse button. Drag the mouse to the ending position, and then release the mouse button.

edit   To make changes to existing information. Editing in a word processor usually involves spell-checking, grammar checking, and making formatting changes until the document is judged to be complete.

Fast Save   An option that reduces the amount of time necessary to save a file during a work session.

file   DOS stores information in files. Anything can be placed in a file: a memo, a budget report, or even a graphics image (like a picture of a boat or a computer). Each document you create in WordPerfect is stored in its own file. Files always have a file name to identify them.

File Manager   A part of WordPerfect that enables you to easily open, print, and locate several files at once.

floppy disk drive   A disk drive that uses floppy disks.

floppy disks   Small, portable, plastic storage squares that magnetically store *data* (the facts and figures you enter and save). Floppy disks are inserted into your computer's *floppy disk drive* (located on the front of the computer).

font   Any set of characters that share the same *typeface* (style or design). Fonts convey the mood and style of a document. Technically, font describes the combination of the *typeface* and the *point size* of a character, as in Times Roman 12-point, but in common usage only a character's style or typeface is described.

footer   Text that can be repeated at the bottom of every page within a document.

formatting   The process of changing the look of a character (to make text look bold, underlined, and slightly bigger, for example) or a paragraph (by centering the paragraph between the margins or by adding an automatic indentation for the first line, for example).

formatting codes   Hiding behind the *formatting* you see on-screen are WordPerfect's formatting codes. When you reveal the formatting codes, you can see these codes on-screen and edit them, if necessary.

function keys   The 10 or 12 F keys on the left side of the keyboard or 12 F keys at the top of the keyboard. F keys are numbered F1, F2, F3, and so on. These keys are used to enter various commands in WordPerfect.

Glossary   A section of the WordPerfect help system where you can find definitions of terms.

Grammatik   A special program within WordPerfect that corrects grammatical errors within a document.

graphic   A picture that can be imported into WordPerfect to illustrate a particular point.

hanging indent   A special kind of indent where the first line of a paragraph hangs closer to the left margin than the rest of the lines in the paragraph. Hanging indents are typically used for bulleted or numbered lists.

hard disk   A nonremoveable disk drive that stores many megabytes of data. Because the hard drive is fixed inside the computer, it performs quicker and more efficiently than a floppy disk.

hard page break   An invisible code that, when inserted into a document at a particular point, tells WordPerfect to begin a new page (even if the preceding page is not full).

header   Text that can be repeated at the top of every page within a document.

indent   The amount of distance from the page margins to the edges of your paragraph. Sometimes referred to as "changing the alignment" of a paragraph.

Insert Mode   The default typing mode for most word processors and text editors. Insert Mode means that when you position your cursor and start to type, what you type is inserted at that point, and existing text is pushed to the right.

insertion point   A blinking vertical line used in some word processors to indicate the place where any characters you type will be inserted. An insertion point is the equivalent of a *cursor*.

jump term   A highlighted term in the WordPerfect help system that, when selected, "jumps" to a related section of the help system.

justification   Controls how the text in a paragraph is placed between the left and right margins. You can left justify (text is even along the left edge of the paragraph), right justify (text is even along the right edge of the paragraph), center, or fully justify (text is even along both edges of the paragraph). Justification is also known as *alignment*.

landscape orientation   Your document is positioned so that it is wider than it is long, as in 11" x 8 1/2". The opposite of landscape orientation is portrait.

leader   Dots that fill the spaces between tab positions in a columnar list.

margin   An area on the left and right sides of a page that is usually left blank. Text flows between the margins of a page.

menu   A list of commands or instructions displayed on the screen. Menus organize commands and make a program easier to use.

mouse   A mouse is a device that moves an arrow (a pointer) around the screen. When you move the mouse, the pointer on the screen moves in the same direction. Used instead of the keyboard to select and move items (such as text or graphics), execute commands, and perform other tasks.

moving text   When you move text, the selected text is deleted from its original location and moved to where you indicate.

numbered list   A numbered list is a series of paragraphs with hanging indents, where the number is placed to the left of all the other lines in the paragraph.

Overtype Mode   The opposite of *Insert mode*. In Overtype Mode, what you type replaces existing characters.

page break   A dotted line which marks the end of a page. A page break can be forced within a document by pressing Ctrl+Enter.

paragraph   Any grouping of words that should be treated as a unit. This includes normal paragraphs as well as single-line paragraphs, such as chapter titles, section headings, and captions for charts or other figures. Pressing Enter or Return marks the end of a paragraph.

point   To move the mouse pointer so that it is on top of a specific object on the screen.

point size   The type size of a particular character. There are 72 points in an inch. Font families usually have only certain point sizes available; if you need larger or smaller letters than your font offers, switch to a different font.

portrait orientation   Your document is positioned so that it is longer than it is wide, as in 8 1/2" x 11". This is the normal orientation of most documents. The opposite of portrait orientation is landscape.

Ribbon   An option that displays at the top of the WordPerfect screen, just under the menu bar. The Ribbon provides quick access to commands that change the way your text is displayed.

scroll bars   Possibly displayed along the bottom and right sides of the Document window; you use scroll bars to display other areas of the document.

scroll box   Its position within the entire scroll bar tells you roughly where you are within your document.

selection letter   A single letter of a menu command, such as the *x* in Exit, that activates the command when the menu is open and that letter is pressed.

shortcut keys   These are used to activate a command without opening the menu. Usually a function key or a key combination, such as Alt+F5, shortcut keys are displayed next to the menu command. To use a shortcut key, hold down the first key while you press the second key.

soft page break   The opposite of a hard page break. This is an invisible code that WordPerfect inserts automatically when text fills a page and a new page must be started.

Spell Checker   A special program within WordPerfect that corrects spelling errors within a document.

Status bar   Located at the bottom of the screen, this displays information about your document.

style   A collection of specifications for formatting text. A style may include information for the font, size, style, margins, and spacing. Applying a style to text automatically formats the text according to the style's specifications.

tab   A keystroke that moves the cursor to a specified point. Used to align columns of text.

text area   The main part of the document window; this is where the text you type will appear.

Thesaurus   A special program within WordPerfect that provides synonyms and antonyms for selected words in your document.

view mode   A way of looking at a document. WordPerfect comes with several view modes: Text, Graphics, Page, and Print Preview.

word wrapping   This is a method that word processors use to adjust a paragraph when you insert or delete text so that it fits between the margins. If you add text, everything in the paragraph is moved down. If you delete text, the remaining text is moved up. Even as you're typing text for the first time, when you reach the right-hand margin, you're automatically placed at the beginning of the next line.

Installing WordPerfect 6

Before you can start using WordPerfect 6, you must install the program on your hard disk. Follow these steps to install WordPerfect:

1 Start your computer.

2 Insert the WordPerfect Install 1 disk in drive A or B.

3 If the Install 1 disk is in drive A, type **A:INSTALL**, and press **Enter**. If the Install 1 disk is in drive B, type **B:INSTALL**, and press **Enter**.

4 If you have a color monitor, press **Enter**. If you have a monochrome (black-and-white) monitor, type **N**.

5 Press **Enter** to select Standard Installation (this is the recommended installation option).

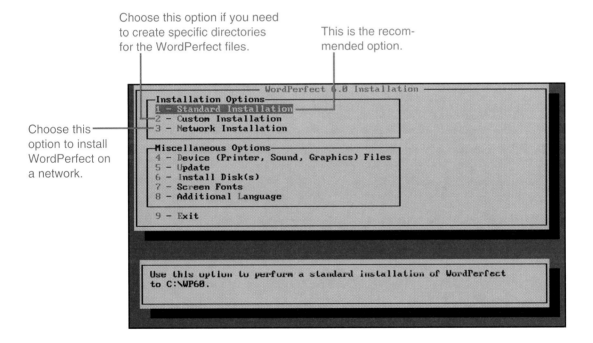

Choose this option if you need to create specific directories for the WordPerfect files.

This is the recommended option.

Choose this option to install WordPerfect on a network.

6 Press **Enter** to install WordPerfect in the suggested directory (C:\WP60), or type **Y** and after specifying a different directory, press **Enter** to continue. If the message, `Path doesn't exist, create?` appears, press **Enter** to create the new directory.

7 WordPerfect displays the number of bytes needed to install. Press **Enter** to continue the installation, or type **N** to cancel it.

135

8 If you are reinstalling WordPerfect, decide how you want the installation program to handle existing files.

9 Press **Enter** to have the C:\WP60 directory added to the path statement in your AUTOEXEC.BAT file. This allows you to run WordPerfect from any directory. Press **N** to bypass this option.

10 If you have an EGA or VGA monitor, press **Enter** to use the standard EGA/VGA driver. If you have an advanced graphics card and you want to take advantage of its features, type **Y** and highlight the graphics card you have. Press **Enter** and **Y** to install the selected graphics card. When prompted to install a second graphics card, press **N** to continue or **Y** to install a second graphics driver.

11 If you do not want to install a printer, press **N** to bypass this screen. To install a printer driver, press **Enter** and then highlight a driver from the list. (Printers marked with a diamond are not included with the program disks. Contact WordPerfect for more information.) Press **Enter** and **Y** to install the selected printer. When prompted to install a second printer, press **N** to continue or **Y** to add a second printer driver.

12 Replace disks when prompted.

13 If you do not want to install a fax, press **N** to bypass this screen. To install a fax, press **Y**. Press the number of the fax driver you wish to install, and press **Enter** to install the fax.

14 If you do not want to install a sound board, press **Enter** to bypass this screen. If you want to install a sound board, press **Y**, and then highlight a sound board from the list. Press **Enter** and **Y** to install the selected sound driver. When prompted to install a second sound driver, press **N** to continue or **Y** to add a second sound driver.

15 Replace disks when prompted.

16 Enter your registration number when prompted to do so.

For information about starting WordPerfect, see Part I.

Index